customs of the people Iduarte meets along the way, as well as penetrating observations about regional Mexican temperaments, mores, and family relationships. His fellow Tabascans are lovingly portrayed as scornful of death, fatalistic, vociferous, bold, and violent, in contrast to the less tropical Mexicans, who act and speak with more restraint.

The author has a rare talent for remembering a young boy's perplexities as he ponders half-understood adult references to racial and sexual matters, and he has a genius for capturing the essentials of the Mexican character and culture.

THE AUTHOR: Andrés Iduarte was born in 1907 in Villahermosa, Mexico. After studying at the National University of Mexico, the Sorbonne, and the Central University of Madrid, he received his Ph.D. degree from Columbia University. From 1952 to 1954, he was Director General of the National Institute of Fine Arts in Mexico. He is currently Professor of Spanish-American Literature at Columbia University, where he has taught since 1939. Professor Iduarte is the author of several prize-winning Spanish works, including a short novel and studies of Simón Bolívar and José Martí.

THE TRANSLATOR: Professor James F. Shearer is Chairman of the Department of Spanish and Portuguese at Columbia University. He is the translator and editor of Angel del Río's *The Clash and Attraction of Two Cultures: The Hispanic and Anglo-Saxon Worlds in America.*

Niño

CHILD OF THE MEXICAN REVOLUTION

Andrés Iduarte

Translated and Adapted by James F. Shearer

PRAEGER PUBLISHERS

New York · Washington · London

PRAEGER PUBLISHERS
111 Fourth Avenue, New York, N.Y. 10003, U.S.A.
5, Cromwell Place, London S.W.7, England

Published in the United States of America in 1971
by Praeger Publishers, Inc.

© 1971 by Praeger Publishers, Inc.

All rights reserved

Library of Congress Catalog Card Number: 72–128099

Printed in the United States of America

Contents

v

Translator's Preface

Mexico has had three popular revolutions.

The first of these was that against Spanish domination, headed in 1810 by a priest from the village of Dolores, Miguel Hidalgo. The struggle was continued by another village priest, José María Morelos, and by civil and military leaders until complete victory and independence from Spain were achieved in the year 1821.

The second revolution was for constitutional reform. It was led in 1853 by Benito Juárez, who promulgated the new Constitution of 1857, triumphed over his internal enemies after a long struggle, and later, from 1862 to 1867, fought successfully against the French Intervention and the imposed empire of Archduke Maximilian of Habsburg.

The third of Mexico's revolutions, that of 1910, commonly called the Mexican Revolution, is the one with which we are concerned, and the one of which the author of this book was a frightened, bewildered, if withal fascinated, observer. This was not, like the American Revolution, a political struggle against a foreign power; rather it was a civil, socio-nationalistic struggle against an autocratic, firmly entrenched oligarchy.

Such an oligarchy was personified in General Porfirio Díaz, who for some thirty years (1876–80 and 1884–1911) had ruled Mexico with the strong hand of a dictator. Not only had he perpetuated himself and his clique in power, but, through his policies, or lack of them, he had fashioned and adroitly consolidated a social structure adverse to the long-range well-being and healthful development of the nation. I say "long-range" because General Díaz, during his rule, established a truly impressive record of economic development and political stability, although these were accomplished, more often than not, by brutal and conniving methods. He attracted millions of dollars in foreign investments, improved communications through an expanded and more efficient railway system, developed mining and industry, modernized and greatly beautified Mexico City. Unfortunately, such spectacular and headline-catching accomplishments, while they made him greatly admired at home and abroad, actually had the effect of making the rich of the country richer and the poor poorer and did little or nothing to alleviate the many long-standing social problems clamoring for solution.

Francisco Madero had long sought, through democratic means, the establishment of a government responsive to the real needs of the country. These peaceful efforts having proved of no avail, he asked the Mexican people to join him in armed revolt against the dictatorship of General Díaz. The unseating of the latter by Madero in 1911 can be called the political beginning of the Mexican Revolution and of a decade of bitter, bloody civil war. Many of the most important figures involved in this struggle appear in the pages of this book, and are briefly identified in the Glossary. In general terms it can be said that this was a struggle between conservatives, past and present adherents of Porfirio Díaz, and revolutionaries, those opposed to him and his practices. This left ample opportunity, of course, for members of one or another of the above groups to fight among themselves and liquidate each other, if necessary, to further their ends. .

But it must not be presumed that these calamitous, violent, and bloody events constituted the essentials of the Mexican Revolution; they were, at best, only sorry aspects of its attempted implementation. The Revolution was much more than a simple succession of revolutionary governments. Its political and social ideals were expounded in the Constitution of Querétaro in 1917. From the standpoint of its ideological bases (not too skillfully elaborated, unfortunately, because many Mexican intellectuals, who would have been the logical architects of its program, remained largely aloof from the movement), it was a widely based and popularly supported revolt mounted for the redress of a long list of pressing social grievances. The elimination of these social and economic ills was going to be attempted through, among other things, the establishment of a generally more democratic political system, with restrictions on self-perpetuation in public office and curtailment of the activities of the military establishment, the Church, and foreign capitalists, especially in the area of subsoil (petroleum and mineral) rights. In other, related areas of social reform, the revolutionaries sought the right of workers to strike, the elimination of a caste system based on massive landownership, and the abolition of the state of virtual peonage that system had created among the dispossessed and disfranchized Indian population.

The revolution with which Americans are most familiar, their own, had a clearly defined beginning, with the Declaration of Independence in 1776, and an end, with the defeat of the British troops at Yorktown in 1781. The author, at several points in his narrative, asks, "Had the Revolution triumphed?" Many political historians, both Mexican and foreign, have for some time been, and are today, repeating his question, although in somewhat different terms. They ask, rather, "Has the Revolution ended; that is, is it dead? And, if so, shouldn't it be buried?" Those who call it defunct point to its many frustrated aims and as yet unaccomplished goals; those who consider it still viable, while they are willing to concede that there have been numerous shortcomings, hasten to stress the Revolution's indisputable attainments in the areas of agrarian reform, labor legislation, education (particularly in the reduction of illiteracy), and the rehabilitation of the Mexican peasant. Moreover, they see precisely in the Revolution's unfinished business, in the above and other areas, the imperative for its continuation and revitalization.

The reader will recognize as perhaps the central theme of the book the gradual waning of the child Andrés' untoward admiration for Porfirio Díaz, culminating in his final disenchantment with the former dictator. It should not, however, surprise us that this idolatry lasted as long as it did. Its duration speaks eloquently of the painful dichotomy in political reasoning that tormented many adult minds during the author's time. Among those actively supporting or apathetically tolerating Porfirio Díaz, there were many, like the author's family, who, while they deplored most of his methods and disapproved heartily of many of his acts, deemed them a small price to pay for the political and social stability that his regime guaranteed, particularly in a country with a secular tradition of violence and passion. How often their thoughts must have turned, over the years, to the memory of don Porfirio and his tight political ship, as they witnessed the crimes and mistakes of certain revolutionary figures.

However, as the author notes consistently, he did not have, as a child, the necessary perspective to make sound comparisons and evaluations of the Revolution and its leaders. This he would acquire with time and greater maturity. A child of the cultured aristocracy, the son of a Chief Justice of the state of Tabasco, a nephew of individuals powerful in the ranks of the Díaz dictatorship, he sees the Revolution arrive, suffers and recoils from its violence, and recognizes its errors, as these are pointed out to him by his family and relatives, and finally comes to reject it and despise it. He records, with sensitivity and candor, the racist attitudes and assumptions that suffused his youthful experience.

We watch the evolution of his feelings about people and their ways. Little by little his eyes are opened to the realities that surround him, and, although still besieged by doubt, he gradually becomes aware of the fact that the peasants risen in arms are justified in their aspirations. He views them at close range; he visits their barracks and later, in the capital, attends school with boys who are the sons of revolutionary leaders and with others of the poor classes.

In this slow, evolving comprehension of the new social realities, his father's conduct and words play an important role. Although a highly placed public official of the old Porfirista regime, his father is a professor of philosophy and fully capable of recognizing the justice of the popular cause, as well as the merits of certain of its leaders, notably Francisco Madero and Venustiano Carranza.

The boy studying in Mexico City is no longer the child born in Tabasco. When he finally removes don Porfirio's picture from the wall of his room and hides it behind a chest, he performs a symbolic act. He has finally come to realize that the covetousness, greed, and venality of certain of the Revolution's false and opportunistic leaders did not mean that the Revolution itself was corrupt, but they did mean that some of its figures were. He now knows that these faults represented, in many instances, failures of men rather than principles and that they resulted from the moral surrender of leaders who, too often impelled by motives of self-aggrandizement and perpetuation in positions of authority, had all but forgotten the rightful recipients of the Revolution's benefits—the Mexican people.

J. F. S.

Niño

My First World

I was born in San Juan Bautista, Tabasco, on the first of May, 1907. Although not a believer in horoscopes, I have always liked the date. The day of workers and of Provençal troubadours, of the floral games of Toulouse and Barcelona, it is a good day on which to come into the world. On my birthday I have often been engulfed by popular enthusiasm for beauty and justice—in Mexico, in Spain, in France. My birthday is always fraught with emotions. But enough of such frivolous reminiscence. The important thing in my life was that I was born in 1907, four years before the fall of the dictatorship of General Porfirio Díaz, and at a moment when Mexico was already beginning to stir politically. Mine was destined to be a revolutionary childhood.

San Juan Bautista was a tiny city, the capital of the province of Tabasco, the most tropical of Mexico, and the one most closely resembling those exuberant panoramas found in the novels of José Eustasio Rivera and Rómulo Gallegos. These were the tropics, with their passion, their bloodshed, their immense rivers—among them, the Grijalva and the Usumacinta, which form a splendid estuary. This was where once the brave —I don't say savage—Indians routed the conquistadors, despite their mysterious harquebuses and diabolical horses. Here too was where the chieftains gave Hernán Cortés the key to the Aztec fortress, in the person of the Indian girl Malinche, his concubine, baptized doña Marina by the Spaniards. This land of vigorous and calamitous history is almost somber in nature, and tragedy supplies its monotonous rhythm.

With a cultural tradition stemming from colonial days, Tabasco has a peculiar, almost unique, tone: it lives by harsh, medieval concepts of honor. Here the duel—a contest between two men, governed by stern laws and from which only one ever returns—is a common practice; here vengeance is both a duty and a pleasure that, even more than in Corsica, tears families apart like Montagues and Capulets. In political struggles emotion overrules doctrine. Friendship is the base governing good and evil. This is a land in which loyalty to a friend is the cardinal virtue and where a friend's disloyalty is inexorably punishable by death. Religious missions never reached Tabasco. Pirates, or buccaneers, did arrive, however, and they— driven off the seas, satisfied, or simply tired, as the case may have been—finally sought refuge and peace pushing inward along the great rivers that excited their daring eyes. Tabasco is still a land of pirates, although now because of its temerity, not its freebooting. The Tabascan—who bears a French or English surname proceeding from the pirates of the Antilles— dies willingly for something in which he believes, and even for something in which he does not believe. There arose naturally then, in the social order, the modern feudal lord and the serf and, in the personal sphere, the unadorned, excessive individual, devoid of artifice, disguise, or restraint.

Situated on one side of the province of Veracruz, open to the world, and the province of Campeche, Tabasco lives a life apart. Its deep rivers, always navigable, link all its towns. Formerly, however, it lived isolated from Mexico City and its plateau because it did not have a single railroad and it was connected with the capital and its environs only by the horses that crossed the swamps and by the flimsy old boats that defied the Gulf of Mexico. Tabasco's population, almost all white, shaded with Mayan and Aztec—for Tabasco was the base and boundary of ancient cultures—looks toward its virgin forests and those of Chiapas and Guatemala—toward those within its confines and toward those on its borders—and the biological frenzy of these lands of exploitation and adventure imparts to the province its unique physiognomy. Scorn of death, a part of almost every Mexican, reaches a high pitch in the typical Tabascan. While the less tropical Mexican moves with a whisper or in silence, the Tabascan makes his mark with a shout and a gesture, without bluster—for the act follows the word. Here life is marked by arrogance, fearlessness, and violence, quite in harmony with great rivers pushing mounds of water across luxuriant lands in fantastic germination, traversing a lush greenness that fairly intoxicates, under a blinding, insolent sun. This is a land of vibrant women, of valiant, virile men. Today San Juan Bautista is called Villahermosa, but blood still flows through its sun-bathed streets.

Naturally it was only later that I came to know the physical and psychological Tabasco of which I am speaking here. I was born, a tiny human bundle, on a steep little street that afforded me my first panorama. This was in a house on Encarnación Hill, on what seemed, to my childish eyes, an almost vertical street in the center of town. Until I was three, I viewed my whole world through two windows with thick bars: the little house of doña Adela Mondragón that was opposite, between that of the political boss don Nicolás Pizarro, at the top of the hill, and the large blue house of the Cantoral family, on the corner of Sáenz Street; the telegraph building—a house with red *repoussé* walls that I used to say had had smallpox—which was adjacent to ours, down the slope; and, on the other side, a mysterious orchard that beckoned to me from the tops of its cherry trees, whose branches extended over a high wall, forming a roof over our patio.

Our house was unpretentious, almost poor, with that lack of luxury and conveniences—and that exquisite cleanliness—of the coastal provinces of Mexico. I enjoyed it very much: I liked to observe the steep street from the windows; invade an unused room where my father kept a large, old broadsword and various shotguns; go to the patio and look over the curb-stone of a very deep well that reflected my image and bathed my face in a cool, refreshing current of air; press my forehead on the green water-jar cabinet in a corner of the dining room; half-swim every day in a large basin in the bathroom; or bathe in a large washbowl that I used to fill with ducks, small fish, and little rubber boats, out in the shade of the cherry trees. I recall that they bathed me there late in the afternoon on the hottest days. But I have not spoken as yet of my greatest pleasure: that of stretching myself out on the black flagstones of the entrance hall—whose open doors allowed free passage of air—and placing my cheeks on them, one after another, and then my chest and finally my back, trying to escape that suffocating heat.

My human world was even better: it consisted of my father, my mother, my maternal grandmother, my three sisters, my nurse Paula, my maternal aunts Cristina and Socorro, and my maternal uncle Carlos. And a little parrot also had a place in that world, no less than my family.

My father had a tiny little parrot, as jealous of his affections as any woman could have been. When he returned home from work, the little parrot, from her perch on the bars of the window, would emit a strident cry and fly down quickly. She always took her place on a corner of the table, between my father, who sat at the head, and my mother, who sat at his right. She remained there on guard, ready to peck my mother if she ventured to move her hand toward his. And for us to kiss him or ride on his legs, Paula, Inés, Lorenzo or some one of the servants had to take her away.

"That damned parrot," Paula would grumble, "one of these days I'm going to wring its neck."

Lunch over, my father would rise slowly and go to his room to take his siesta in his net hammock. Although the blinds were half-closed, the sun's glare made an oven of the room. The little bird would jump from the table to a chair and, aiding the faltering march of her crooked feet with her wings, follow my father. Grasping a strand of the hammock with her beak, she pulled herself up and onto him, taking care not to scratch him with her claws. She would pause on his forehead and scratch his head with her beak, rhythmically, almost scientifically. With this my father would fall asleep, despite the heat, and savor his tropical siesta until the big dining room clock, striking three, awakened him. While he slept, the parrot would climb up to the ends of the hammock, and at times even ventured as far as the hooks from which it hung. But if we children were to peek into the room, she would hop quickly to the floor and chase us. I would run away frightened, lifting my red and purple smock up to my waist.

This little parrot, so covetous of my father's affections, was a mysterious being in my eyes—half-human, half-diabolical. She amused me greatly but I was afraid of her.

Born shortly after the death of another son, I was the last and only male child of a small and comfortable family. My childhood was a happy one. The son of an essentially good and sweet man who was, moreover, fond of teaching, I remember my youth as a period that was spiritually joyful and rewarding. My material needs were amply met, and I have no recollection of blows, reprimands, severe punishments, capricious prohibitions, corrections at table, nor religious obligations. I grew up doing and saying whatever I wished. My father was a teacher of logic, psychology, and ethics in the Instituto Juárez and professor of civil law in the law school of the same institution. I learned about his profession from early childhood because I played with Spencer, Comte, Giddings, Ferri, and Lombroso building houses and bridges, castles and fortresses.

I have taken pleasure in stating that my father was a teacher; I take none in saying that he was a judge. He was District Judge and Chief Justice of the state of Tabasco for many years. My only thoughts on this were that he had the misfortune of being poor, and of having children to support while bearing the burden of being a judge, a cross heavier than that of Jesus Christ. But I can say now, with pleasure, that he was a very humane judge, a real judge. It would have been impossible for that good and sweet man to mete out with cruelty, as did so many others, the punishments prescribed by the penal code. "The white blackbird of the judiciary," one of the leaders of the liberal revolution in Tabasco called him. And indeed he must have seemed a "white blackbird" to the rebels who fell under the arm of the law. There was much of the saint in my father. He died fifty years ago and still now, awake or asleep, I feel that his tender eyes are upon me.

My mother was a beautiful, blond, blue-eyed woman, almost always serious and melancholy, and marked by a sort of ineffable sadness. She had never studied eugenics, but she bathed me every day and took very good care of me. I have only the most pleasant recollections of her. The only thing that later displeased me about my parents was hearing them discuss certain mysterious matters in which the name of a woman invariably came up.

I have a keener recollection of my grandmother and of my nurse Paula than of anyone else, because they spent the most time with me. My maternal grandmother was a diminutive old lady of a little over·sixty years, gentle and sweet like bread and honey. She had a far greater influence on me than anyone else. One generally magnifies the size of things he saw as a child: what he imagines as having been a large village square was actually only a little plaza; what he recalls as an enormous man was in reality an insignificant little fellow. Just the opposite occurs with my dear grandmother. Across the years I recall her as very tiny, standing about a yard high—a true miniature. Perhaps this is because I could do whatever I wished with her. I remember her blue eyes, clear as two drops of water; her white hair, parted in the middle and held tightly in the back in a small white chignon. I recall her white arms, flaccid and traced with blue lines: with childish disrespect I used to play with the loose flesh that hung from them.

It was she who made my imagination roam through other worlds. She introduced me to my grandfather, her deceased husband. I remember his tall frame, his sorrowful face, his long, romantic locks. I knew him, I knew him as a part of a fantasy transcending reality, because she carried him within herself, alive, animate. But actually he died when she and her children were very young. At the age of three I heard a most dramatic and cavalier story from my grandmother, as I recall —although possibly from others as well, since my grandfather Manuel Foucher is a legend in Tabasco. Political poet, a man overflowing with love for the people; liberal, anticlerical, he was assassinated on Ampudia Bridge while governor of my province. Every inch a man, he succumbed standing, defending himself. He was an authentic, not formal, Christian: he died saying "Forgive them, O Lord." In the character and life of that man there was a contradiction to be observed frequently in Tabascans: he was sensitive and tender but he lived in an atmosphere of violence and unbridled virility. For all his sensitivity and tenderness he held to the terrible, legitimately Tabascan principle: "Anyone who insults me I'll hit; anyone

who hits me I'll kill." In the ambush where he died, twenty
men jumped onto the bridge under which they had been hiding and fired on him and his friends. Mortally wounded and
covered with blood, he drew his pistol. He fired and the leader
of the assassins fell dead, shot through the head. Such a bellicose end did not prevent his regaining his gentleness nor dying
with a Christian phrase on his lips.

My grandfather's social rebelliousness was the product of a
difficult childhood. The son of a beautiful, virtuous, but un-
fortunate young woman, he knew poverty, hardship, and hard
work from his earliest years. My grandmother used to tell me
that he died for the people, that he always distributed his salary among the poor and that, at his death, his total wealth was
sixteen *pesos*. Although his culture and his setting were of
more modest proportions, my grandfather, in his poetry and
in his life, was markedly like the Cuban revolutionary José
Martí. It was not without significance that, as a political exile,
he had experienced the First Cuban War of Independence.

My grandmother, on the other hand, did not spend her
childhood in poverty. Although the daughter of a rich man,
she married for love. Her relatives spoke continually of blood
lines and aristocracy, but she paid only scant attention to such
matters. She had other virtues. I heard that she had been a
pupil of the famous Mexican jurist don Justo Sierra O'Reilly.
For her time and provincial milieu, she was a cultured woman
—she read good books and spoke French. After her husband
died, my grandmother, much like Salomé Ureña of Santo Domingo, the famous educator, established a small school in the
sierra of Tabasco. The government later retired her on a pension. Then her three daughters were married: the eldest to the
most influential lawyer of the province; the second to my
father; the third to a doctor greatly revered throughout the
state. Her son turned out to be extremely intelligent but was
too much a bohemian to take anything seriously, and at the
same time was too poor to get to the cultural centers of the

country where his talents would have been appreciated. Finally, my grandmother had twenty grandchildren to enrich with her accounts of two saintly lives.

My grandmother was my guardian angel. When I used to draw with crayon a circle of strange figures on the black flagstones of our hall and suddenly, seeing myself surrounded by "sorcerers," break out in tears, to the great amusement of everyone, it was she who rescued me; the two or three times that they locked me in the bathroom she was my indignant liberator; and she was the one who collaborated with me in my daily executions—through the use of three dolls I kept for this purpose—of Emperor Maximilian and the two Mexican generals, Miramón and Mejía, who died with him at the end of his rule. My sisters and the servants were the ones who told me about don Trifón, the bogeyman, and about the "sorcerers" that so obsessed me then and later on.

It was also my grandmother who informed me that there was a very good God seated above the clouds, and she taught me the Lord's Prayer. There were three pictures in my house, vestiges of the fervent Catholicism of my paternal grandmother, whom I never knew: one of the Guardian Angel, another of the Holy Infant of Atocha, and one of the Virgin. However, I received very little religious instruction. I recall one night when my only devout aunt was telling me things about the Virgin. When I arrived home I asked my mother something about the Holy Lady. She answered me by pointing to the Virgin of the picture; but I didn't want her to talk to me about that one but about the one in the sky. Not being exactly able to explain to her that I was referring to the original and not to the picture, I said I was talking about "the Virgin with guts," meaning the flesh-and-blood, authentic, tangible, real Virgin. My materialism reached such extremes that I pictured the Virgin in Heaven with intestines and all. The fact is, no one practiced religion in my home: they were not married by the Church, did not have their children baptized, and no one went to Mass. My grandmother had a deep faith in a God she imagined to be very good, and she died in that faith; but she never spoke to me of Christ the King. I used to hear my mother and my aunts assert their belief in the survival of the soul, but that was the end of it. They taught me neither the Ten Commandments nor the seven deadly sins. I had no idea what the catechism—that other children recited like so many parrots—was. Later on, when I was some nine years old and we were in Campeche, my father used to read and explain to us certain pages of the Gospels. He spoke to me of Christ as a man as good as my grandfather.

Once, however, I did kiss the hand of the Bishop of Tabasco, of whom my father was a very close friend. Occasionally they would come to the house together, arm in arm, or gesticulating a great deal as though arguing about something, but laughing a lot the while. The servants would take out two wicker chairs for them and they would sit for hours in endless conversation. One day, as I drew near to my father, he said to me, "Kiss don Leonardo's hand, Andrés . . . There, that's right."

Don Leonardo Castellanos made me kiss a big ring he was wearing, patted me on the head, and remarked, "Go now and play, you little heretic."

My nurse was Paula, a Negro or mulatto, possibly a granddaughter of Africans who had come to Tabasco with the pirates fleeing the Antilles, or perhaps of Negroes who had crossed the Gulf at the time of the so-called Staircase Conspiracy in Cuba. In my child's world, Paula represented the street —sin. She loved me very much because I was a clever and not overly mischievous boy. I never caused her much work and learned faithfully both her stories and the nicknames she assigned to all the family friends. She made me call a bald doctor "my uncle Wig," because of the toupé she said he wore. She made me shout "long live France" to don Tacho, an indigent old man who had been a soldier in the struggle against the

French Intervention, and whom my aunt Cristina had taken into her home. The children used to drive the old man, who was almost maniacal with patriotism, nearly out of his mind with this cry. Finally, Paula concocted the most daring nicknames for Monchito Becerra, secretary to Governor Abraham Bandala, my neighbor and the best friend of my childhood. She was famous in the town for her waggish tongue and her slanderous disposition. I think she loved me very much, but she did teach me scurrilous language, and malicious tongues said she did evil things to me. To judge from how much I loved her, these things—whatever they were—must have seemed very good to me. She bathed me two, three, sometimes four times a day with Reuter's soap. I recall how wonderful she smelled, and I think too of her fresh, black, hard, and shining skin. I liked her skin even better than the cold flagstones in the hall of my house.

Such was the scene and those the characters who peopled my first world. I enjoyed comforts, but had no idea that others lacked them; I had my own servant, without realizing this to be a special privilege.

2

Prelude to Revolution

My stage widened at the age of four when we took a trip to
my cousins' hacienda. Our boat ploughed through the great
tropical rivers, I saw alligators sunning on the banks, observed
legions of monkeys caressing one another in the thickets and,
for the first time in my life, felt the mystery and enchantment
of the forest. I came to know the sea, the blue and violent
waves of the Gulf of Mexico. My cousins' property was truly
marvelous: thousands of gracefully slender coconut trees, serene peacock flowers, and a succession of thick groves. On
one side lay the swollen river; on the other the howling Gulf.
We always went down to the water before it got too hot.
Alone, or at times accompanied by my grandmother, I explored the small saltwater lagoons dotting the beach. Later,

holding my father's hand or atop his shoulders, I would enter the water to be buffeted by the waves. On land my greatest discovery was the crabs—they were everywhere in endless profusion, even in the house: yellow, black, dark purple, red ones—and I amused myself a great deal with the smallest, those less prone to bite. I vaguely remember the loading of copra on the banks of the river. I still carry a vivid impression of don Manuel, the manager of the property, a tall, curt, lame Spaniard. Nor can I ever forget Pancho Gómez, the trusted associate of my uncle, an individual half-servant and half-relative who reproduced endlessly and thus supplied the Foucher families with domestics, half-brothers and -sisters, half-servants. I recall, too, that the peons on the estate always greeted us respectfully, with a great flourish of their large palm hats. Once, with my aunt, I entered one of their small houses and observed the unpaved floor, the makeshift furniture, in short the poor world of which I really knew nothing. But now when I think of La Montaña, as the estate was called, my mind harks back to a mysterious little window, a kind of latticed niche in my room, and I still don't know what it was nor why it had been made. No one ever explained this to me. My childish head struggled a long time to unravel this enigma, and today the estate and the little window are one in my memory.

As for the Revolution, although this outing must have taken place during the Madero period, I detected no signs of it anywhere. The fact is that the Revolution, as it would have been recognized by a child, did not reach Tabasco until 1914.

Nevertheless, Mexico was shaking. It is my impression that my father was no longer the Chief Justice, and that he busied himself only with his classes and with the affairs of his law office on Juárez Street. The province was no longer governed by the famous don Policarpo Valenzuela—don Polo, friend of my family, owner of the house in which I was born and of half of Tabasco and who, Paula said, maliciously, had a picture of the devil painted on his back. My sisters and I took this for gospel truth, and you can well imagine our anxiety when we caught a glimpse of the old governor's posterior! It was about this time that don Francisco Madero came to Tabasco. I'm not positive that I really recall him or whether, instead, I have fashioned his slight figure and smiling face in my imagination as was the case with my grandfather. But I do indeed recall Dr. Manuel Mestre Ghigliazza, the Maderist Governor of Tabasco. He was a poet, a physician, and a journalist; he was physically impressive and the idol of the children, who acclaimed him when he passed through our street mounted on a horse of imposing stature. One day Paula and I saw Madero on the Parade Ground, and the women of the populace applauded him and threw him kisses. Shortly thereafter it was learned in Tabasco that he had been assassinated. The atmosphere was charged. I am in a position to speak of a few antecedents of the tumultuous events of 1914.

Early one morning there was a hammering on the door of our house. I used to sleep in the same room with my parents, and I heard someone tell the latter that my uncle, the attorney Juan Martínez, the husband of my aunt Cristina, had been wounded and that they were taking him to his home. Did I peek through the blinds? Was what I thought I saw a figment of my imagination? I recall a bloodcurdling picture: a hammock covered with a red counterpane, carried by several men with muffled faces. Perhaps, as I have suggested, this was only the fruit of childish fantasy, because it was absurd to bring the wounded man to my house, which lay well distant from the road one had to follow to go from the river to my cousins' home. I remember little of my uncle in his lifetime. He was a tall, robust man, with a large, impressive mustache and an absent-minded air about him, but most kind and gentle to his children and to us. However, I do remember him in death. The white shroud and the candles left an indelible impression on us. The story I heard related there was even more impressive than the wake.

My uncle had been the most influential lawyer and politician in Tabasco during the dictatorship of don Porfirio Díaz. Throughout his lifetime he was one of those most attacked by the opposition despite the fact that, like my father and all the family, he was a layman of liberal persuasion. My childish eyes did not see him as he was painted by his enemies. My mother loved him very much. After my aunt Cristina married him, my grandmother, my mother, and my aunt Socorro—the youngest sister—lived with them as they would have in their own home. Literally an army of the poor ate there. Attached to the family as extra members or hangers-on were a large number of persons whom I recall only most vaguely: Camila, Lupe, Concha, Atala, and the Verdejo sisters. These appendages of the feudal family were called *crianzas*, closely resembling the Spanish ladies of the queen's wardrobe, who served in the house but on a basis of equality, or almost so, and who were more like companions than servants. One of them played the guitar and composed verses and songs, and she used to sing, among other things, a supposed dialogue between one of the girls and my aunt, who opposed her engagement. My aunt paid for the burials, marriages, and various social affairs of her *crianzas*, who called her, with great affection, "doña Cristinita," adding an endearing diminutive to her name. Frequently she, my grandmother, my mother, and my aunt Socorro would wrap themselves in their black shawls and leave the house in whispers to spend the night away from home. They had gone to minister to someone ill or to keep vigil over a dead person, a relative of the *crianzas*. The relationship was one based on protection and tenderness from top to bottom in this social hierarchy, and of unconditional compliance, gratitude, and faithfulness from bottom to top.

There were always a large number of these supernumeraries about but they were never mistreated. When one of the boys, possessed by the spirit of the street, hit one of them, he received a reprimand or there was meted out to him, in retaliation, the same blow he had struck. To my certain knowledge stocks were prohibited as a method of punishment on my aunt's properties, although in wide use in almost all of Tabasco; the peons were never beaten, nor were children and pregnant women obliged to work.

"We are landlords," I often heard my aunt comment, "but not executioners."

Moreover, there was an extraordinary human warmth in my grandmother, in my aunt Cristina, and in her sisters, and one could only love them. Neither extreme rebels nor advocates of any political doctrines (that would have been impossible for women of their period and environment), they did much to smooth away the harshness of that patriarchal, feudal, and medieval life. At that time my aunt was a beautiful young brunette, with large passionate eyes. Within the inevitable limitations of provincial life, she was a cultured woman, with an intuitive understanding of all things. And above all, it seems to me, she injected a certain nobility and altruistic enthusiasm in everything she thought, said, and did. There persists in Tabasco the living legend of her goodness, linked to that of her parents. She was a woman formed in, and destined for, tragedy. When she was ten years old she found her father dying in the street. From that day on she was a second mother to her young brothers and sisters. And in the full bloom of her youth they took her one day to her dying husband. Following this she lived for months in a darkened room, given over completely to her desperation, but without once imprecating her husband's assassin. And when the judge questioned her about his death, she said she was not interested in having the killer punished. Seeds of civilization and culture, sown by who knows what chance wind in the fields of violence, my aunt and her brothers and sisters always said that were a relative or a friend to kill another man, whether in self-defense, in a duel, or in the frightful, traditionally bloody quarrel of Tabasco, "Better they had killed him . . . your grandmother preferred her sons to be the dead, never the killers."

My uncle was treacherously shot to death while General Victoriano Huerta was in power. He had been inactive in politics since the fall of don Porfirio, and, almost blind, he had been thinking of going to Mexico City for treatment. Before doing so, however, he wished to visit one of his properties, the sugar mill of Santa Rita. The new manager, a man of suspicious background, quarreled with him. Some attributed the dispute to personal differences of the moment; others said that he was simply seeking a pretext to carry out something long planned. Without my uncle's being able to defend himself, half-blind as he was, the manager fired several shots that wounded him in the mouth and throat and he fell to the ground. There still resound in my ears the words he managed to utter from there, words I have so often heard repeated. They were a judgment that could only spring from manliness in the throes of death.

"Don Marciano, this is not the way men are killed."

Real men, he meant, are killed face to face without unfair advantage. My uncle was a man of proved personal valor, known for his scorn of death, which, in the Tabascan milieu, was and continues to be the attribute most highly esteemed by everyone. His attacker fled. As soon as my uncle was taken to San Juan by his followers, my cousin Juan, less than fifteen years old, set out in a motor boat in pursuit of the assassin. After the legends of personal valor of my grandfather and my uncle, I was beginning to hear of another new and vibrant legend: that of my cousin, the oldest of the Foucher grandchildren. Etched in my memory much like an heroic engraving is the account of the apprehension of don Marciano, who was fleeing as fast as he could in a kayak, armed to the teeth, but who, on seeing the son of his victim, surrendered without a struggle. The hard-bitten Tabascans who went to offer their condolences to my cousin told him, "You should have killed him on the spot." My uncle died three days later from an unstanchable hemorrhage.

At this time I began to learn that there were two groups in the world that pursued each other to the death, that there existed a fury against the rich and the powerful, even against the good.

My cousins left the large house in which they were living and came to live opposite us. The Foucher clan drew closer together and garnered strength from misfortune. Around the corner lived our Carpio cousins, the children of the doctor; but we were on much more intimate terms with those of the attorney. My aunt Cristina was the oldest of the sisters, and her children the oldest of the new generation. Hers was the manorial house. From that time on, I lived in very close contact with the entire family group, and many of my opinions and values were formed under their influence.

We had a servant by the name of Límbano who had formerly worked for them. He was an Indian boy with the frozen look of his race, but with an affectionate smile on his lips. He used to take me on excursions to. Juárez Park, to the Parade Ground, and to the Playón, a level spot covered with grama grass and lush green vegetation on the banks of the Grijalva River; or he played with me in the house. He was one of my most beloved servants. I don't recall just what he said to me about don Porfirio and my family: something to do with politics and wealth, but in any event I repeated it to my mother. I only remember that one night my father, very nervous, talked alone with Límbano. I must have sensed that it had something to do with my gossiping, because I hid behind a chest. My father noticed me, made me come out, and gave me a slap across the face.

"That's for being a gossip—a blabber-mouth," he said to me.

For me this constituted a tremendous punishment, since my father had never struck me before. The fact is, Límbano was a rebel already engulfed in the rising flames of revolt. In 1917, at the height of the Revolution, I saw him one day in the Cruz Verde neighborhood and went to speak to him. He was ragged, shabby, and very thin, but he was carrying his rifle. I accompanied him to his barracks, located in Esquipulas Church. He said he would come to see me at the house but he never did, and we were told that he was killed in battle shortly afterwards.

My companions called me Hothead because I had a bad temper and was quick to come to blows. My first victim was Bruno, the son of Pancho Gómez, my uncle's servant. I struck him once and they punished me. Another time when the poor boy was enjoying a tropical siesta on the sidewalk, a little friend of mine who lived nearby began to urinate in his face.

"Wake up Bruno," he said to him, "it's raining."

"What do you think, *niño*, that I don't feel how nice and warm it is," he replied, opening his smiling eyes.

This bad prank of my neighbor's cost us the most violent reprimand from my father, but I can only say in self-justification that in this, and in many other things, I was dominated by the feudal atmosphere in which we lived. I soon had another servant by the name of Martín. One afternoon he took me to the Merino Theater to see one of Toribio's pictures. When we came out I was sleepy and in a bad mood and began to hit him for who knows what reason—perhaps without any. Martín was a strong boy, larger than I, with tiny, lively, joking eyes that irritated me a great deal. He defended himself without hurting me, rather laughing at me the while. This irritated me even more. A man who was standing in the doorway of a small, poor house nearby regarded me with anger, with hate-filled eyes such as I had never seen before, and shouted, "All that is going to end come the Revolution!"

My father found out at once what I had done and gave me one of his severest looks. After thundering at me he admonished me not to strike the servants, pointing out that they were boys like myself, my equals and especially his, because he was the son, and I the grandson, of a carpenter of Teapa; because when young he had been as poor as they and had delivered milk and fodder and I don't know what else in his village. That impressed me greatly, but I'm not sure whether I liked it or not. I rather think not, because by now I considered myself an "aristocratic" boy. But I was never to forget, ever, that I was the grandson of a carpenter. Years later, that was to become a source of joy to me—the discovery of my connection with the people. But the truth is that all my childhood was a sort of alternate ebb and flow, an uncertainty: socially I found myself in a confluence of forces, in a hybridism that a child was incapable of overcoming.

3

Ancestry

I came to know about our ancestry through family visits and chats.

Near my house there lived some dressmakers, relatives of my father and of the same name. Whenever I was a nuisance at home my mother would send me to their house and tell them to give me a "keep-me-here." They would give me whatever they had at hand and so keep me with them. In this way I learned that the apple, a rare fruit in Tabasco, was called a "keep-me-here." They were three sisters, two of them widows. The third, the most wrinkled of the lot, was unmarried or, more accurately, an old maid. My aunts Ricardina, Chole, and Pepita were evident proof of my modest family connections. Ricardina had a son, Pánfilo, owner of a millinery

shop, and several daughters: one of them sewed, as did their
mother, and two had studied and were teachers in the Normal
School. My aunt Chole had an only son who worked as a
marine mechanic on the rivers far from San Juan. In her house
I learned that not all my relatives were ranchers, lawyers, or
doctors. Moreover, my two cousins were dark-skinned, and
from this fact I became aware that perhaps we all had some
mixture of Indian blood. In that house everyone loved me a
great deal; after all, I was the son of the cousin who had been
successful. But I recall that one day they told me, in a strange
tone of voice, that I was not rich, that I lived from what my
father earned, that I shouldn't think we were wealthy nor be
presumptuous. I had another relative, Sílfide Limón, so poor
that she could be considered almost a servant.

As a matter of fact a part of my father's family was extremely poor, among the poorest of the sierra of Tabasco. My
father had been able to study thanks to a scholarship; he was
one of the best students of his time and was appointed a
teacher in the primary school. He later took a law degree, obtained posts in the judicial system, and chairs in the Instituto
Juárez and in its Law School. He came, finally, to occupy
high positions, but always refused those of a political character offered him by the dictatorship, of which he did not wish
to seem a supporter. He married my mother, who was also
very poor, the daughter of a pensioner of the state treasury,
but who boasted surnames highly regarded in southeastern
Mexico; she was the sister-in-law of a powerful man, and she
was blond. Although at first blush it might not seem so, her
blondness was very important. The wealth of the Martínezes,
the blueness of eyes and greater whiteness of skin of other
relatives of Tabasco and Campeche, the social position of all
the Foucher clan, and the prestige of my maternal grandfather's name were going to result in a social status that would
fix our childhood firmly within the framework of counterrevolution.

It would seem that my paternal ancestors were Basque or Irish peasants who came to Tabasco about the beginning of the nineteenth century. My father's family must have been unconcerned about their genealogical tree, or perhaps work on the land or in the shop left little time to ponder it. As for the Basque provenance, I think I deduced this from my family name, with the help of a brilliant but rather eccentric professor who taught me Roman Law in the School of Jurisprudence in Mexico City and who was an expert on heraldry. In any event, as a boy I heard it said that my great-great-grandfather spoke a strange language, that he was Irish or a descendant of Irishmen and that, until the people Hispanicized it, he had an English name. Or then again perhaps he was a Basque, and that was the strange language he spoke.

But the idea of an Irish or English origin pleased me during my adolescence. I lived the phase of personal valor, inevitable in the youth of every Tabascan, and I had it that my forbears on my father's side were Antillean pirates. I still recall an enormous portrait of my great-great-grandfather that my father had discarded in an old trunk: hard eyes, angular features, clean-shaven, and with a fine, rugged jaw. I learned, too, that he had been very strong, and that on one occasion, with a single blow of his fist, he knocked out a man who had attacked him with a knife. I found out also that he hunted ocelots with a machete. But all this was really superfluous: in order to establish bellicose antecedents it was sufficient for me to recall that the family was from Teapa, whose cemetery, it was said, was a veritable lead mine, so many were the dead from gunshot wounds buried there. My father's family first engaged in blacksmithing, carpentry, and agricultural pursuits. They were a very honorable people, very virile, very solid, without political interests. But there were the inevitable blood mixtures, and as a result diversification and variety began to appear in that family too, including prosperity and political influence.

The fact is my father also had well-to-do relatives, although they were more generally peasants or ranchers than were my mother's. Some went far through their talents and efforts; certain ones thrived from higher prices for the cacao or coffee they planted; still others effected advantageous marriages. My father's was such, in a strictly social sense, since his wife was the daughter of Governor Foucher. Certain of my father's cousins were proof of this hybridism of which I have spoken. I recall four old rubicund, apoplectic ranchers. They used to bring servant girls to my house from their estates, under ostensibly respectable circumstances, and then later, on some pretext, usually that of exchanging them for harder-working ones, would take them away. Someone found out that they were bringing them there, to transfer them later to another of their ranches as soon as they were pubescent, then to violate and enjoy them at will, while incurring no obligation to them or to their parents. There was a small scandal in the bosom of my family; one of the girls was rescued and my house ceased being a mousetrap or fattening station. This custom was not by any means unusual among the landowners of Tabasco, nor did it prevent their being greatly revered by the "best people."

On the other hand there were certain of my father's kin who were quite the opposite, for example my uncles Casiano and Pablo Pombo. My uncle Casiano was a rancher, although not a particularly prosperous one. He was a quiet family man, lived a retiring life and, in moments of crisis, took his cue from Pablo, who, of the two, possessed the more dynamic personality. This uncle Pablo was really an oddity: badly dressed, bearded and slovenly, he couldn't fail to impress me, accustomed as I was to neatness in people, even making allowance for tropical relaxation in such matters. I remember him as always being excited and exasperated and continually using strong language. As a matter of fact he came to my house only during periods of crisis, of which there were many. His life was a succession of adventures. One day I learned that he had been arrested, and this was the first time I had ever heard the word "incommunicado." This happened while Victoriano Huerta was still in power. This audacious and valiant uncle Pablo, with only fifty men, entered a village by surprise and drove off the garrison. But they caught him and later brought him to San Juan Bautista. It was rumored that they were going to execute him on the road under the law of flight, in a contrived escape attempt. My father intervened with the governor and was able to save his life. After he was brought to the San Juan Bautista jail, his meals were sent to him from our house. I recall that, still recalcitrant, he communicated with my father by sending him notes hidden in the rice left on his plate. I don't know whether they acquitted him or whether he was freed with the triumph of the Revolution. I felt a great attraction toward this rattle-brained uncle, but, at the same time, I was somewhat afraid of him. No sooner did he reach the house than I would run to spy on him through the cracks of the doors. I was in the presence of a mystery: he was the revolutionist.

My father's family, as is evident, was a potpourri, but its dominant tone smacked of the small village. The peasant stuck out of them even in a certain penchant for thrift, in a propensity for saving which frequently reached the point of the picturesque. I heard that my paternal grandmother kept a small box of coins handy and from this she would loan herself money. She would take a coin for this or that and as soon as she could would put it back with this consecrated formula: "A coin you gave me, and a coin I return." One of my father's brothers had some land in Teapa. An uncle of his was the park guard, that is to say the gardener. This perhaps helps one understand his fondness for the people and his many friendships with humble folk: with Ciriaca, who made corn tortillas in Tamulté, and to whose cabin we used to go on Sundays to eat large thin ones called *totopostes;* with Ricardo, a stevedore, whom my father used to invite to drink a Berreteaga brandy with him; with Mayito and with Mundo, sellers of lottery tickets; with the seer Rosario; with the Indian Nato, the poet from Atasta.

Contrasting with the evident humbleness of my father's family were some very old and rather stuffy traditions on my mother's side. Here the greatest merit lay in the French name, and not simply because it was French, but because it was illustrious. She came from a family reaching Campeche and Tabasco probably during the first half of the nineteenth century, a family that had distinguished itself in public affairs since the first generation. Esteban Foucher was secretary of the government of Tabasco in 1846, and as such was one of the leaders in the defense of San Juan Bautista against the invading squadron commanded by the North American Commodore Perry, who failed to capture the town. It is also said that the Fouchers had been expelled from France because of their liberal views, that the family contained generals and writers, and that they were close relatives of the wife of the French writer Victor Hugo. Others contend that they came to Tabasco from Mexico City and that they were collateral descendants of one of the distinguished professors, a doctor of the University of Paris, who in the sixteenth century taught in the Colegio de Santiago Tlatelolco. A French, Victor Hugo-Sorbonne origin? I wouldn't know. But I do know that seven Fouchers came to Tabasco, three sisters and four brothers, one or two of whom moved to Veracruz and there left a numerous family; that my great-aunt, the daughter of one of them, and with whom I conversed during the whole of my adolescence, spoke of New Orleans as the point of origin; and that this port is the seat of one of the oldest branches of the French Fouchers.

The principal concern, however, was not to be noble, but to be white; not to be Indian, but to be descendants of the masters in the conquered lands. My maternal grandfather must have passed, during his youth and owing to his ancestry, through a period of marked concern for aristocracy: the most serious error of his life was to have been seduced during the time of the French Intervention, despite his liberal views, by the mellow accent of the French General Achille Bazaine and the blond beard of Emperor Maximilian. This was the period in Mexico when no one wished to be Indian, least of all don Porfirio, whom his wife almost turned white with various face creams and hair lotions and who, at eighty years of age, except to a discerning anthropologist, no longer seemed the son of the Indian girl Petronila Mori. A French, English, or German name and a pair of blue eyes were the undisputed letters patent of aristocracy. Spanish blood was also much admired but was so common that it gradually lost caste. Spanish surnames lost their distinction as the Indians took the names of their conquerors.

As for the family of my maternal grandmother from Campeche, its position stemmed rather from wealth than from distinguished lineage. One or two members of the Paullada family, of French descent according to my uncles, but more likely Catalans or Valencians, came to America, where they became prosperous through the cultivation of logwood or in the development of salt pits. One of them, or one of their sons, returned to Spain, and I believe that from him come all the Paulladas of Chiclana, of Cádiz, of Jerez, and of Puerto de Santa María. Others suggest that the relationship is older and that the Paulladas of Campeche and those of Andalusia spring from one of the families of shipowners who were involved in the discovery of America. An uncle of mine from Campeche, my grandmother's brother, still had some extremely old parchments and portraits depicting a group of ruffed, solemn, and heavily bearded gentlemen. We know that my grandmother's father, both blond and wealthy, was one of the liberal leaders of Campeche.

Further enhancing the French name, the memory of the Paullada wealth, and the blue eyes was the distinguished social and political position of my aunt Cristina's husband. And later there were the facts that he was a lawyer like my father and that my other uncle was a doctor. Academic titles are very important in Spanish-American society. The sum total of these privileges was then: an aristocratic, distinguished family, one of the first families.

Moreover, in my mother's family there was a certain tone of authentic aristocracy that was in no way based on race, money, color of eyes, or origin of name. There was a devotion to reading and a concern for undertaking heroic enterprises and aiding the destitute. I must admit, of course, that in our house we read both the good and the bad, the great and the mediocre, without much discernment or refined literary taste. But, after three generations in the midst of the forest, the Spanish and French romantic writers were discussed, and at the height of the Revolution the works of Spanish-American authors like Gutiérrez Nájera and Rubén Darío occupied the place of honor in our evening gatherings.

In any event, the situation in the various parts of my family as regards social position was, to say the least, a varied and complicated one. On my parents' side we had brunette relatives like ourselves, and at the same time there were those mixed with humble families. However, they were rich land-owners, within the meaning such words had in that economically poor world. Also in both branches we had relatives of more humble origin; but they were blond. Were we of the *white* race? From our color we could have been; from our features, who knows? We can't be certain because our genealogical tree—as is the case with the great majority of Mexicans —is a melancholy little shrub, marked by prunings and enormous scars, that can be traced, at least in some of the branches, only as far back as the great grandparents. We are—and here is a consolation for the racists—of the *whitish* race. The Spaniards take me for a Spaniard, the French for a Frenchman, but, were an anthropologist to examine me, it is quite possible that the satisfaction of my racist friends would go down the drain. And such would be the case with many others: the eyes somewhat slanting; the skin of some of my kin perhaps too cinnamon-colored; the forehead in some instances very narrow; the hair frequently in very tight curls. We may have Spanish Semitic blood or perhaps native Mayan. But we three Foucher families enjoyed a "great peace of mind"—as I heard it put—because we knew that at birth we didn't show Mongolian spots. This, according to racist obsessions, was a guaranty that there was no mixture with any of the conquered races.

The avalanche of the Revolution was beginning to rumble. In the long run our family was not going to be classified by my father's liberal ideas on social rehabilitation, by his culture, or by his nobility. There are things that transcend man's desires and intentions. What was going to classify us was his marriage to Adela Foucher, considered an aristocrat, and the fact that he was the brother-in-law of Juan Martínez, one of the wealthiest and most influential men in the ranks of the Porfirista dictatorship. My father was a simple man, of humble family origin. By both temperament and conviction he was a populist, a lover of the people. He lived without luxuries, without frivolities. Far from being devoted to the Church, he was a militant anticlerical, a Freemason, a disciple, philosophically, of the positivists don Gabino Barreda and don Agustín Aragón, a natural reaction to the excessive religious indoctrination imposed on him by his mother. Throughout twenty years of judicial activity he never had a cent. This means that he made no deals with the landowners to give grounds for hatred among the dispossessed. And that is not all: in the Instituto he molded some of the most precocious youths of the time. I often sat on the knees of such future leaders as Rafael Martínez de Escobar, Francisco J. Santamaría, and Manuel Bartlett. Neither were we going to be pigeonholed by the tradition of grandfather Foucher, living and strong as it was. Social position and fairness of skin placed the Foucher clan on a counterrevolutionary course.

4

The Revolution

They put me in school at the age of six. I attended the private lay school of Professor Gonzalo del Angel Cortés, which was very near my house, at the top of Encarnación Hill on Hidalgo Street.

My attendance at the school widened my horizons. I met the village blacksmith, and his dirty and indigent appearance, as well as his ill-humored face, covered with soot, made me reflect that there were badly paid people in the world who suffered greatly; and he prepared me too for the many other angry faces that I was soon going to see. Also my relations with the neighbors multiplied, as I encountered them on my way to and from school.

Every day I would go to the bakery at the corner of Sáenz

Street and push my nickel through the mysterious opening on the counter. Then the baker would give me a hot hard roll, or a golden sweet roll.

At times my father would take me by the hand and we would go to the pharmacy of don Elías Díaz, where I would buy gum drops and listen to the conversation of the men who met there with the druggist.

We also went to a variety store where there were always a large number of men. Some of them would go into the back room to have drinks with the owner. His wife, doña Chona, was a very gay old lady and more foul-mouthed than her husband. She had some small dolls with pins stuck in their heads, through their hearts, and between their legs. One day when I discovered them in a shoe box she gave me a shove and cursed me. Years later people told me she was a witch and a bawd.

But then, too, my own home was the scene of marvelous discoveries and childhood experiences. There were days when it thundered a great deal, and our mother explained to us that "Daddy God is grumbling." Suddenly a large clap of thunder would sound, and such a torrent of water would fall as seemed likely to break the tiles of the roof. My mother and my sisters, in fantastic-looking bathing suits, would run to the middle of the patio, or stand under the downspouts, that were gushing great streams of water. There was a fresh, luscious smell from the damp earth, broken branches of the cherry trees covered the ground, and my small world trembled. After the bath, still oozing water, we again ran and played our childish games:

> San Juan, San Juan,
> San Juan was born on Friday,
> On Friday was born San Juan. . . .

Finally the hot tropical sun reappeared and a half hour later we were roasting again.

At night my explorations extended to the corner, where I joined a group of other boys. However, being very weak physically and a little shy—a mamma's boy—I preferred to pass my time with the swarm of cockroaches—big fellows, black and hard as stones—that fluttered around the galvanic arc lamp flickering above us, and which I liked fully as much as the crabs on my aunt's estate. I made them fight with one another, run races, go up and down slopes, and jump over obstacles.

I don't recall whether it was then or before this that I again came in contact with nature. I remember that we went to Teapa, the mountain village where my father was born. One traveled by river to El Rosario, my cousin Manuel Tellaeche's estate, and from there to Teapa on horseback. I recollect only the home of my uncle Pedro and the park where my uncle Efrén, the gardener, planted flowers in the form of letters and words. It was on the return trip, at El Rosario, in the midst of a banana plantation, where I again encountered civilization: in the form of the telephone that connected the estate with the town. At that time we also went to another estate, Las Delicias, that belonged to my cousin Josefina Tellaeche. There, in front of its great lagoon, I heard frightening stories about the alligators that emerged from it to pursue people and from which it was possible to escape only by running in a circle. And finally they showed me the tracks left by their enormous claws in the damp earth. Over a green and humid plain I took my first elegant ride in a coach that had been brought from the capital. Then we returned to San Juan Bautista, and before my vacation was over I was face to face with the Revolution.

It was the thirty-first of August, 1914. Various dismal-looking battalions passed through the streets. The soldiers seemed very tired, very sad, and very dirty. They were quite different from the way I remembered them, singing gaily on the parade ground of my town. The bugle sounded otherwise than I had ever heard it before. We children were ordered to get into the house and not show ourselves, even at the windows. That day I didn't have my hot chocolate with my puff pastry, my sponge cake, my butter cookies, or my marvelous Tabascan bread that my friend the baker brought us, fragrant and hot from the oven. Something out of the ordinary was happening. My house began to fill with people who closeted themselves with my parents in the interior rooms. I was seven years old by this time and nothing escaped me. I remember distinctly a conversation between my cousin Manuel and my father, in which the former said,

"I think you should leave tonight."

"I've done nothing to anybody, the people love me. I have no reason to flee," my father replied.

"But they are going to treat the righteous like sinners. These are not times for fine distinctions. They can easily make a mistake, confuse you with someone else. Many people who don't know you, who don't know how honorably you have acted, are coming from the villages."

"I assure you that they will do nothing to me."

A short time later my aunt Cristina sent for my father to discuss the matter of leaving. My grandmother and my uncle Rogerio Carpio, the doctor, were present at the meeting. He was a good and sensible man, completely removed from the world of politics. His opinions had always had a decisive influence on the other three leaders of the Foucher clan. My father returned home still undecided. It was my uncle's opinion that, in order to play safe, and to avoid unpleasantness for the women and children, the prudent course was to leave San Juan that night.

More troops passed by the house, and before nightfall we heard the first shooting. The door of the house had been secured with heavy beams and with an iron crosspiece that was never used ordinarily. During the night there was a knock on the door. It was my cousin Manuel, still insisting that we should leave, and he was finally able to convince my father.

The shooting continued. Nevertheless, my cousin and my father went out, and when they returned the firing had ceased, and they began the preparations for the trip. I don't know whether the city was already in the hands of the revolutionaries, or whether a part of the garrison had mutinied and had been put down. What I do remember is that, while still in the house, my father assured us that we could count on "all kinds of guarantees." I never forgot the phrase.

Night had fallen by now when we set out. We twenty Foucher grandchildren gathered at the door of our house, and the women arranged the group for the departure. They and the children walked in the center. My father, my uncles Rogerio and Patroclo, my cousins Juan, Manuel, and other persons carrying carbines protected us.

I remember vividly looking back with sadness at the house in which I was born. I turned my head time after time, not wanting to give it up. I recall it in the middle of that unforgettable night, such as I had never experienced before, a night full of both enchantment and terror—my first night of adventure. Ah, my little house, set on that steep, terraced walk that we Tabascans call—and rightly so—an escarpment, near the edges of which I used to run the wheels of my velocipede until I became terrified at the thought of falling on the gray rocks below! The telegraph pole on which I pressed my cheeks to cool them, my ears eager to discover the mysterious secrets running along the wires! The thick bars of my window, to which on Sundays my father tethered his great white horse, on which he used to gallop as far as his small farm, Tierra Colorada! Left behind in that house were my balls, my velocipede, my slates, my pencils and my marbles, to say nothing of Maximilian, Miramón, and Mejía, my three favorite dolls. I wanted them to collect and load all of my belongings. I recall that my greatest concern was to take with me a plaything I had hidden behind a door, I don't remember whether a hobbyhorse or a wheel. An irretrievable part of my heart remained there. One cycle of my restless, feverish, and agitated Mexican life was coming to an end and another was beginning, this one to end perhaps in death.

The Foucher clan descended the long, low hill. We were going toward the river on Lerdo Street. Here I took leave of another beloved spot, the carpenter shop of don Darío López, where I used to go to see them work the lathe, where they gave me small boards to play with and where, finally, they used to call me "Attorney Shavings," obviously thinking of my father's profession and the occupation of my grandfather, or of my being as talkative as a shyster lawyer and as thin as a wood shaving. We turned at the corner into Aldama Street, emerged and took Constitution Street. I said farewell to Puerto Escondido, a narrow, slum-like little side street that interested me very much. It harbored a mystery that I would solve later on. Along there we saw a dead man. We had come across another on Aldama Street, lying on his back, his arms outstretched. We continued on in the direction of Juárez Park. At the corner of a wide thoroughfare, later called Madero Street, they hurled a "Who goes there?" at us.

"People," answered one of our group.

"What people," asked the soldier.

"Peaceful people . . ."

One of our men moved toward the troops and talked with them. We continued on toward the Grijalva River, through the dark, gloomy night. I remember our passing along the river bank: darkness, whispers, the sound of grass crushed by our footsteps. Here there was a circus, the Beas circus. My family was afraid there might be troops or rebels there and spoke of the danger. We approached the canvas cone in panic, but passed by without incident and finally arrived at the immense Grijalva, where they put us on a boat. The boats of Campeche, called *canoas campechanas* are excellent for river navigation, and even defy the perils of the Gulf. They put us to bed in the hold and I must have fallen asleep, because I remember nothing more. They told me later that there was shooting on the banks of the river and it was feared that the boat would be fired upon. Even so, my cousin Juan refused to go to the hold and went to the deck in defiance of the danger. Once again I was hearing of his temerity, which so captivated and enraptured my childhood.

After a four-hour trip we arrived at Frontera, a modest little port. My father had a niece there, but I don't remember exactly what she was like nor her name. I recall only vaguely that she was stupid, perhaps retarded. She had married an old man, always very well dressed, and they had a very fine house. My parents commented on this marriage, arranged by the girl's mother, and I began to understand how the "good marriages" were agreed upon. My mother also had a relative in Frontera. He was pleasant and always most affectionate with us. We were supposed to call him "uncle," but they never told us ʼanything precise about the relationship. He kissed my mother and my aunts, and we asked ourselves with persistence what he could be to them. When he left he kissed them again. I don't know exactly how they explained to us that he was the son of my grandfather, but not of my grandmother; that he was my mother's and my aunt's brother, but not their brother. Suddenly I did not understand the riddle: for they had always told me that when two people got married, a little basket was lowered to them from Heaven, containing a baby. Then I acquired a most important piece of knowledge: that men have children by different women. I realized that I had been lied to, and many disquieting thoughts began to stir in my head. My "uncle" Pipo was the fruit of one of my grandfather's peccadillos after his marriage, but my grandmother had always loved him, and he returned her affection in kind.

From an improvised wharf we took the boat that would carry us to Carmen Island in the state of Campeche, following the marvelous river system of Tabasco. It was a river boat like a two-story house, constructed on a flat horizontal base and propelled by enormous red blades that beat the water and made an infernal noise. We children thought it wonderful and enjoyed playing on the decks and seeing how that great wheel churned the waters of the river.

We had some terrifying encounters on the boat. Members of the Huertista government were fleeing Tabasco and had embarked with us. To accompany them was, quite frankly, to risk one's life, but by now there was no turning back, and we left at the middle of the afternoon.

During the night we saw a kind of blaze in the distance. What could it be? It turned out to be the light of another boat. My aunt Cristina and my mother discussed this in the prow of the vessel, seated near the rail. I overheard my aunt invoking God, asking and expecting something from Him. Suddenly there was a disturbance, strange preparations, running back and forth, orders.

"All women and children to the rail!"

We were there when our boat, the "Clara Ramos," and that of the revolutionaries, the "Mariano Escobedo," came together.

"Long live the Revolution! Long live Carranza!" they shouted, raising their rifles menacingly.

Rifles, pistols, red-banded palm hats . . . and some churlish looks. I heard some rough words that neither frightened nor shocked me, since Paula had already taught me all of them. I recall that a large number of people jumped onto our boat and seized several of the gentlemen traveling with us. Imagine a bunch of poor wretches seizing aristocrats! This was what surprised us children as we gazed from underneath the skirts where we had taken refuge. There was one soldier who gave a lot of orders—I learned later that he was a sergeant—a man with a mustache and beard, completely covered with hair, who shouted at us continually while he beat the floor with the butt of his sinister-looking rifle.

"Don't worry, children, we don't eat people, indeed we don't," he thundered.

The poor fellow, who must have been a sincere revolutionary, was indignant upon seeing the panic-stricken faces of the women and children, who took him for a real bandit. My mind must have been strongly conditioned against rebels because, despite his protestations of friendship, he failed to inspire me with confidence.

My aunt Socorro, who always displayed great presence of mind, was the only one to show no fear.

"The people love and protect the Fouchers. The revolutionaries cannot harm the daughters of don Manuel Foucher," she declared.

This statement produced no effect one way or another. Despite the admonitions of my grandfather, the terrible, unrelenting exploitation in the lands of Tabasco had continued. His name produced no reaction, no emotion of any kind in them. The poor country peons had surely never heard it, but the revolutionary chieftains had. However, the great store of love and sympathy left by a pure heart and a selfless life grows silently, transcending time and death itself. My aunt Socorro had been right—we were all protected and respected.

We children and the women were given orders to go into the staterooms. I, with my mother, was in that of my aunt Cristina. She was seated on a hamper that she was guarding carefully, and which probably contained money or some sort of valuables. Suddenly I asked, in a voice filled with alarm,

"And my father? Where is my father?"

I had seen him on the deck speaking to a rebel.

"Where is my father? Hasn't something probably happened to him?"

All of us, my sisters and I, were questioning in unison, fear reflected in our voices and in our eyes. Our mother tried to calm us.

"No, children, he went to the other boat with a friend of his, with the man who was on deck. He will return."

This was really to get "wised up": my father was the friend

of a rebel, he had gone to the other boat with a rebel, he mixed with revolutionaries. Was such a thing really possible? The idea resounded in my head: my father was the friend of revolutionaries, he actually had dealings with them. When he returned we breathed a sigh of relief. We imagined he would return without his clothes, perhaps even without his head. We showered him with kisses. There was no question about it, I thought that to be a revolutionary was the same as being a thief or an assassin.

Later I learned that he had gone to the other boat to convince the revolutionary leader, who wanted our vessel to return with all its passengers to San Juan Bautista, that this, besides being senseless and unnecessary, might well result in excesses of no conceivable use to their cause. It was obvious that they were not beasts because they acceded, imposing a single stipulation: that everyone leave his hiding place, and that those they considered guilty be handed over as prisoners. I have been told that the list later drawn up, where many names figured as the result of the inflamed passions of the moment, was reduced to seven through the intercession of my father and other persons. But perhaps this was only because, as others suggested, the more prudent found good hiding places in the dark corners of the boat. My father was of humble origin, he still had the unaffected manner and language of his class, had been diligent in his services to the people, and was a friend of José Preve, then a young man, who commanded the Carrancista boat. (This Preve after having run the gamut of mistakes, was years later to die in a noble and fearless expedition in Venezuela, against the dictator Juan Vicente Gómez). A few men were taken to the other boat as prisoners. It was related that three of them were bound and hung up like so many bunches of bananas and thus taken to San Juan Bautista. And you can be sure that a few days later they were all shot. My uncle, Manuel Ferrer Vega, military chief of the defeated federal troops, continued calmly playing his game of chess in the smoking salon of the boat, while the revolutionary soldiers searched it from stem to stern. He had served in the dictatorships of both Porfirio Díaz and Victoriano Huerta; he was a friend and follower of don Félix Díaz—the unsuccessful nephew of don Porfirio—and later he would be a general in the rebel camp; but in peace or in war he was an extraordinarily good man. A Huertista colonel on board put on a broadbrimmed hat, pulled it down over his eyes and squatted on the ship's staircase, clutching a pistol under his blouse and prepared to kill before surrendering. Either no one recognized him, or he mattered less to them than he supposed. Don Pico, son of the old Díaz governor, was hidden, I believe, in a large hamper by my aunt Socorro.

In any event, despite the frightened faces of the women and children and the angry grimaces of the men, we were able to continue our trip.

5

Términos Lagoon

Carmen Island stands at the entrance of beautiful Términos Lagoon, swollen by the waters of the two great Tabascan rivers emptying into it—an ample marine shelter with two outlets to the Gulf on either side. The island makes the lagoon a refuge like the covert of a bull ring. In the central part of the island is Carmen City or Laguna, as it has been historically, although improperly, called: it is a splendid natural port, a happy, pleasant, and hospitable town.

Here the state of Campeche begins; here the passion of the Tabascan is diluted and the bonhomie of the Campechan appears. Without doubt the Spanish adjective *campechano*, meaning "frank," "cheerful," "cordial," is derived from the character and disposition of those seamen and shipbuilders who set out from Campeche to explore the world. The Campechans preserve this character and disposition in every sense of the word. The name of their land, coming I believe from the Mayan words *kam pech*, has given the language a word as noble and cordial as the land itself. Cultured, gentle and mundane, the influence of the Campechans in Tabasco has been in every way beneficial and civilizing. The most intellectually distinguished Tabascan families almost always have a blood or school tie with Campeche: either one of their children studied in the neighboring province, or one of their forbears was a Campechan. The cross-breeding of the Campechan and the Tabascan joins the grace of the one to the energy of the other.

Through my grandmother we came to know places and people. That big, five-story house was where one of her stepmothers (her father, like a good Campechan, married four times and fathered eighteen children) shut her up when she was a little girl and kept her on bread and water, and from the balconies of which she, a rebellious child, threw the same bread and water. That other house was the one my great-grandfather gave so they could establish the *lycée*, which still stands. All those on that side belonged to don Victoriano Nieves, a Campechan even more wealthy than her father. And on that corner, mounted on a burro, don Esteban Paullada delivered his first speech against the gringos at the time of the 1846 invasion, and there he set out on the road that led him to the colonelcy of the patriot forces. My grandmother informed us of these things standing on the wharf, raising her tear-filled blue eyes and pointing with her tiny little finger.

We went to live in a very large house that our relatives had prepared for us. There were a number of such relatives in Laguna because it was the seat of my mother's family. Everyone knew us. My grandmother marveled at having gotten back to her native land. Every day she would receive an endless number of visitors or would walk the streets of Laguna with her tiny, quick steps calling on her old acquaintances. Relatives and friends were of all types and social classes: my great-grandfather had been a patriarch, the protector and benefactor of people of every category, from rich to poor.

She had a grown-up nephew there, stand-by of the older members of the family, delight of the children, and very affectionate and good to everyone: this was my uncle Chico Ramos, another victim of the Revolution. He had been wealthy but this was beginning to change. One day I came upon him surrounded by his children, a discouraged look on his face, spreading out on the dining-room table countless rolls of bills of various denominations that over night had become so much waste paper. My grandmother also had a stammering, paralytic sister in Laguna named Salomé, who regaled us with unintelligible speeches. Although still very young, I was greatly interested in linguistics. A servant would have had me believe that Hermelindo, the typographer uncle of my Martínez cousins, had learned to understand the language of the chickens. One of my greatest desires—I was eight at the time—was to understand both the language of the chickens and of my aunt Salomé. My grandmother also had a brother. He was very poor, a teacher of French in the city *lycée*, very intelligent and picturesque, full of Andalusian grace like his relatives from Jerez and Cádiz; but everyone called him "crazy Paullada." This was understandable, among other things, because of his literary proclivities, quite unusual among his neighbors, and also because he had fathered twenty-eight children by a single woman—his wife. He was the custodian of the family titles, of the parchments, and of the ancestral portraits. He was, himself, an ancient silhouette: tall, taut, somewhat solemn, simply but carefully dressed, reminiscent of the gentlemen of the old Spanish provinces.

The house we occupied was immense. All of us cousins played together, climbing the trees of the patio, and at times fighting among ourselves. There I began to realize that all was not sweetness and light and that the Foucher clan was divided by frivolous differences. The Martínezes were the only rich ones; the Carpios were the fair-skinned; but we boasted of being the children of the professor, of the good and honorable judge, of the learned teacher, of the most charming man of San Juan Bautista. From then on the members of the clan lived in alternate stages of rapprochement and estrangement, of quarreling and making up, like so many cats and dogs, but always as one in moments of grief or danger. It was, indeed, the classic clan.

Despite the divisions already existing among the older cousins, and the blows that we younger ones exchanged, life in that enormous ant hill was very enjoyable for us. It was not quite the same for our parents. For one thing, they had the problem of feeding us and precious little with which to do it. I recall the daily menu: banana soup, baked green bananas, fried bananas, banana purée, banana tortillas, and sun-baked bananas. In the richest banana region of Mexico this was the logical and only solution. However, our elders also made an effort to amuse themselves. There was always a big party at night, with the amusing fabrications of my uncle, the French teacher, and experiments in spiritualism, in which some members of the family had great faith. They believed in the possibility of communicating with the spirits and sometimes tried to do so. Two of my relatives knew how to enter into a trance. They would grasp the slate pencil, make insistent appeals to the elected spirit who finally possessed them and then, with shaking hand and bulging eyes, would fill page after page with incredible speed, while we stood about in silent astonishment. Through those seances there passed all the beloved beings and famous personages, among whom the most entreated—after July 2, 1915, the date of his death—was don Porfirio. That was a time when communication with the living was not enough. It was necessary to have the dead, whose spirits were everywhere, tell us what was going on in Tabasco. However, I don't think they proved to be very good messengers: they came when summoned, but made the same statements as the living. And through the living, news of the Revolution in Tabasco reached our gatherings—it was ablaze.

One day my uncle Carlos Paullada, the French teacher, came hurrying to the evening party and, showing the whites of his eyes and running his finger across his throat, said, "They killed Pepe Valenzuela yesterday. They say that when they got to San Juan Bautista they tortured him, skinned his feet, and made him walk several kilometers to the cemetery, where they shot him up against the wall."

He then turned to my father:

"And so they were going to respect you as a professor, because you were good to them, and because your father was a carpenter? I have also learned that your house was sacked by the troops from Chontalpa; that your house and office have been made into stables; that your pictures and portraits are rolling about the streets of the city; that your books have been sold at ridiculously low prices or thrown on the trash heaps, where they are picked up by anyone wanting to read, or what will you."

"To hell with the rebels," exclaimed my rich uncle Chico Ramos, with a bonhomie that made it ambiguous as to whether he approved or disapproved of them.

News reached us, too, that the poet Andrés Calcáneo, a precursor of the Revolution, a follower of Madero, a dreamer and a romantic, had been a victim—like our house—of an excessive act, some confusion or intrigue, and had been shot, unjustly assassinated. I can still hear the voice of my mother extolling his exemplary courage: "He asked for paper to write to his wife Eva . . . he leaned on a tree. . . ." We also learned at that time of the death of another man, a landowner, but a generous one, according to my family. He was caught and shot, it was said, by one of the illegitimate sons he had fathered on one of his ranches.

I was not at an age for subtle distinctions nor reasoning, but I hated those who killed and plundered. I listened to bitter complaints and impassioned accusations—but not from my father: he listened and remained silent.

The Foucher clan broke up into three groups. For some time I have no recollection of my grandmother. Did she go away? Did we? I recall her later in a house in Laguna, that of my cousins the Martínezes. Was it before or after my trip to Campeche? I remember that she suddenly felt ill, and that later I went to her hammock to kiss her. Then one morning she summoned all her grandchildren, large and small, and took leave of everyone, resigned, almost smiling. She died while my cousins and I were playing in the patio. We had made a bonfire that we had converted into an oven, placing a tube above it like a chimney. We were having a gay time throwing into it all the bugs and insects we could lay our hands on—shouting and laughing the while—when my cousin Juan came out and told us very seriously to be quiet, and he told us why.

My grandmother's death saddened us greatly, and made us more serious than we already were. We were quiet children, self-engrossed, our eyes absorbed by the tragic spectacle of the Revolution. Her death added an element of precocious grief, and the strange chatter of my uncle Carlos Paullada filled my mind with fears and superstitions. He said, for example, that she had died because a black butterfly had entered the house.

When my grandmother died I believe we were living by ourselves, in a modest little house beside that of my uncle Chico. My job was to run errands, and I bought the milk from a family who were friends of ours.

"You Tabascan bandit," they used to say to me jokingly.

But I took this very seriously and would answer, "A Tabascan yes, but one of the robbed, not one of the robbers."

I was clearly marked as belonging to the counterrevolution. I was no less marked by my father's honorable history. I knew many details of his scorn for substantial gifts, his refusal of everything except his salaries as a teacher or Chief Justice, of his independence in his relations with Governor Bandala and don Polo. I knew that my father had been a sort of institution in Tabasco, custodian of the small widows' and orphans' fund. When we would go out together on the street, a thing we both enjoyed very much, we frequently met someone who would ask, pointing to me, "Is this the heir, judge?"

"To what? I have no idea to what," my father would respond.

"To your good name, judge, a thing more valuable than money."

Or "to your honesty" or "to your good deeds" or something of the sort. It's quite understandable that I couldn't forget this. Therefore, in the store where I bought the potatoes, when they happened to give me a cent too much in change, I would cross the town to return it; and it was the same with the milk: I refused to accept a drop more than I had paid for. Honesty had become pride: "What's mine is mine, and what's yours is yours." A typically conservative ideology. I knew I was one of the robbed. It was at this time that an uncle of mine said that my father felt the voluptuousness of his honesty; there was no doubt that I did.

That was the period of the smallpox epidemic. The war had been followed by hunger and then by pestilence. There were yellow flags everywhere, marking the stricken homes. Little by little they began to surround us. First there was one at the corner house, and I avoided going that way. Then one appeared on the other corner. Finally there was no way to avoid passing near them: one morning I saw that a yellow flag had been hung in front of my door, on my neighbor's house. Smallpox was everywhere. Mexico was struggling against it, but there was no reliable vaccine with which to attack the disease. We were vaccinated many times, but the inoculations didn't take. My parents' anguish consisted in not knowing whether the vaccine they received was spoiled, or whether the bottle was part of a good supply obtained earlier. My mother bathed us every day in the patio, setting hygiene against contagion, and made us a delicious cold drink from tamarind, which had been prescribed, I don't know on what basis, as a preventative of the disease. I was terrified about smallpox. When not busy at my job as errand boy, I used to play in the patio of my uncle Chico's house. There was a plum tree there, and I knocked the fruit down by throwing stones at it. In order to improve my aim I would threaten myself: "If I don't knock that one down I'll catch smallpox." Or when I tried broad jumping: "If I don't jump to *there* no one will be able to save me from smallpox." The disease was my incentive, my obsession, my interlocutor. It terrified me to observe the daily succession of funerals, the majority of them modest, with primitive, unpainted wooden coffins, or with the deceased wrapped, like a *taco,* in a palm-leaf mat. One day, passing by the door of a shack in another quarter I caught a glimpse of the bare, white, dull-looking feet of an old dead woman, surrounded by a group of weeping men. One evening my father wanted us all to go for a walk and we went toward the wharf. There were yellow flags everywhere. My parents returned home very distressed. As for myself, I felt that the disease was entering my body with the very air I breathed. That night, I was unable to sleep, my sensitive, childish head filled with terror, excited by the atmosphere of drama and desolation engulfing the city.

At this time I had my first quarrel of a scientific nature. This was a clod fight with Prudencio, my cousins' servant, over whether or not the *tusas* have a tail. He insisted they did and I disagreed. The *tusa* is a variety of field rat, but I never learned its scientific name nor whether or not it has a tail.

This was also the period of my first sexual restlessness, my first conscious uneasiness in these matters. Because before leaving Tabasco I had already heard my Carpio cousins debate the question of how we came into the world, and I had some very grave doubts about that business of the little basket. In San

Juan, when one of their younger brothers was going to be born, Rogerio, Panchito, and I stationed ourselves at a strategic spot in the patio, to see the basket, which, lowered from the sky, would be entering through the skylight of one of the rooms. We waited in vain. Then suddenly they came out and told us to give up the vigil, that my little cousin had arrived. How had the little basket gotten into the room? They never gave me a satisfactory explanation.

In Laguna I underwent an acute period of discomposure. One evening, in the presence of my uncle Chico, I insisted that my mother explain to me how one came into the world. I shot down all her spurious explanations: I would have nothing of babies being brought by herons, storks, baskets from the sky, or as coming from Paris, Berlin, and the like. She had to dodge the issue and pass the buck to my father: she told me to ask him when he came home. I recall that he arrived, that I asked him, that he answered me, and that I was satisfied; but it's curious that I don't remember just what reply he gave me. Was it the truth, the physical truth, more comprehensible for my eight confused years than any lie?

There were many reasons why this worry was going to increase in Laguna. Behind my house there lived a mulatto girl named Eduviges, the paramour of a North American. I used to spy on them through the cracks in the fence. The gringo chewed tobacco, spat a great deal, and tickled and pinched Eduviges' arms, buttocks, and legs. He also caressed her in other ways that were unintelligible to me. Eduviges twisted about, laughed boisterously, and in turn kissed and bit the gringo.

Then there was another thing: one of uncle Chico's servants, Nicolasa, had a prominent and—as far as I could judge, considering my tender age and lack of expertise in such matters— well-developed bust. I was especially attracted by its erectness and mentioned this to the servant Prudencio. The latter repeated it to one of my cousins, who was in his prime, was sexually sophisticated, very charming and comical. He was always flirting with Nicolasa. He thought my remarks funny and one day, in front of her, he made me repeat them. I did so quite simply. She blushed and became furious with me. I never could understand why.

Also there was a retarded girl who lived near my house, and who used to lift up her dress and tumble about on the ground. It was then, finally, that I realized boys and girls are not made the same, and it's possible too that I made even more important deductions. Later, on my return to Tabasco, I underwent another crisis that was calmed by my moving to Mexico City with its twenty-four-hundred meter altitude, distant from the unbridled surroundings of the tropics.

6

The Flight

We went by sea to the port of Campeche, I don't recall whether fleeing the Revolution or the smallpox. We left the white island, finally taking leave of its crest of coconut palms. We arrived at Campeche with its great stone wharf—in the old days the best on the Gulf. Campeche is the town of southeastern Mexico that has most preserved its colonial flavor, and perhaps the only one in the country conserving the bellicose memory of pirates. Still standing were the thick walls erected to defend the city from their attacks. It was a serene, exceedingly quiet town, facing an extraordinarily green sea. Almost all the people were very white and had extremely blue eyes. The Mexican from other latitudes who comes to the province of Campeche to enjoy the sweetness and serenity of its way of life and the character of its people must perforce imagine himself in another world. There they call the foreigner *mushú,* and all the Campechans seemed like foreigners to me. The same trace of the French pirates remained in Venezuela, where everyone from the outside is called *mosiú,* which, like *mushú* is a corruption of the French word *monsieur.* Because of the piratical and climatic links, all the coastal areas of the different republics of the Caribbean and the Gulf resemble each other more—in accent, cuisine, and spirit—than they do the higher interior provinces of their own countries. For example, we, the Tabascan children of my time, heard more accounts of the two Cuban wars of independence and of the sad transfer of Puerto Rico to the United States than we did of things transpiring in the Mexican capital itself. The Campechans, white, blond, with a seaman's air, bearing Spanish, French, and English names, devoted to culture but also to the drunken carousal, are a mixture of the men of the viceroyalty and of the corsairs. Pirate blood crossed the walls erected by the Spaniards against the incursions of French and English freebooters. Except that a quieter nature and culture attenuated the proclivity to quarreling, worsened in Tabasco by the savage environment.

In Campeche there lived another brother of my grandmother's—she had seventeen—a doctor (a very good man, to be sure, but a loudmouth) in whose house we spent a few weeks. Later, in the district of San Román, in a house the back of which faced the beach, I came to know the marvel of the Campechan sunsets. Then, in another on America Street, a very large one—ten rooms, a garden, a patio, and a back yard—I learned about botany and zoology by observing flowers and insects, hand-in-hand with my father on scientific expeditions to the most out-of-the-way corners of the property. Jasmines, roses, orange and guava trees were my only friends in Campeche, and I talked and laughed with them. Then one day they all died when a swarm of locusts darkened the sky and descended on the town. Not a single leaf or flower remained on the trees. Nature was joining the Revolution to teach me to live without middle-class roots, without attachment to material things, and making me realize that happiness and financial security are always ephemeral.

In that house I amused myself watching Atala take a bath. She was one of the *crianzas* of my Martínez cousins who accompanied us to Campeche. The barracks were at the side of my house. She would step nude under the water jet in the patio, while a mischievous soldier, unbeknown to her and with me looking on as an accomplice, entertained himself by sticking his head up over the wall and gazing at her. Atala caught on later and punished me by showing me her legs, raising her skirts up above her knees. This made me blush, but it didn't prevent me from looking at them.

There was poverty, and especially alarm, in our house. Campeche was beginning to tremble. A Tabascan general, with a very bad reputation among the followers of Porfirio Díaz, arrived there. The curious thing was, however, that no one did anything to my father; on the contrary, everyone came to the house to greet him. I believed—as he did, although the rest of the family did not—that fears arising from the general confusion were being exaggerated. Except of course that the sacrifice of the poet Andrés Calcáneo was still very much on our minds, and my mother was afraid.

We went to live in Lerma, a fishing port and splendid watering place. The rear stone steps of our house extended into the water, and when the tide was up we used to wade in with our parents. In the distance we could make out the sails of the fishermen's little boats. The fish were sold on the beach, fresh, alive, jumping inside the baskets. I don't recall the endless varieties nor their Spanish and Mayan names. My mother prepared the classic *pan de cazón*, the incomparable Campechan dish (corn tortillas stuffed with dogfish). We lived almost exclusively on fish fillets, *panuchos* (small fried tortillas filled with beans, onion, and fish), and kidney beans, bought at the

Puerta de Tierra, the most picturesque gate in the town wall. But not as an epicure nor as a zoologist, but as a boy, other fish interested me more in Lerma: the sharks. They had two frightening rows of teeth. The female sharks interested me specifically because their bellies moved, full of little sharks. The fishermen would nudge them with their feet and make the little animals swimming within stir about. To learn that the mother sharks carried their young in their bellies was a most important discovery. Later on when I observed a neighbor lady, the legends of the herons and the little basket disappeared for good. But what I still couldn't understand was how the babies or the little sharks got into the belly in the first place.

A part of the rebel army was encamped in Lerma and the soldiers, starved to death, came to the house begging for food. I used to go out and give them fish fillets or *panuchos*. This was my first friendly contact with the Revolution. I became a great friend of theirs, and they invited me to their barracks, near my house. Dirty and bad-smelling, their quarters made a great impression on me. On the floor, on palm mats and under filthy blankets, the poor soldiers slept in a heap. They were sad and gentle, the majority from the central part of the Republic: we called them the *guachos*. At night I used to fall asleep hearing them singing a song that began *"Adiós, adiós,* bright star of my nights . . ."* Ever since then a barracks and that song have been synonymous to me. I also learned *"La Adelita,"* *"La Valentina,"* and *"La Cucaracha,"* and learned to sing,

> With the beard of Carranza
> I'll make a *toquilla*
> To put in the hat
> Of General Pancho Villa.

and other much cruder things. But I always liked best the *"Adiós, adiós . . ."* of my friends the soldiers of Lerma.

One day we went from Campeche to Mérida, the capital of

Yucatán. This was the first time in my life that I had felt myself shut up in a railroad car. I don't know whether we moved about so much because our flight was continuing, or because my father was looking for work. We lived by practicing the greatest frugality, and with the little money some of my father's friends sent him.

In Mérida we lived on Sixty-second Street, in a house with an immense patio, shaded by large trees. In that place I became acquainted with roller skates, as well as asphalt, and amused myself by climbing onto the rears of the horse-drawn carriages. Mérida is white, clean, neat, and shining. Spanish cities like Ecija or Cádiz, almost all Andalusian cities, remind one of it. For me the most important things in Mérida were the Peón Contreras Theater—I had never seen one so large—and a store called The Two Faces. I can never forget those two faces, a double profile, on its façade. I was also impressed by the house of another of my grandmother's brothers, located in the fashionable quarter, with its marble stairways, a coach, and Japanese servants. My cousins, a boy and a girl, were extremely conceited: they were very rich, very white, and good-looking, and always wore new clothes, with their hair done up to a T, curled and shining. They never came to my house to play with me. One afternoon they took me to theirs, and I sat on the steps, bashful and out of sorts. I was annoyed by their clothes, their marble steps, and the look of my very elegant aunt, who wore her hair in a sort of teased bouffant style that reminded me of a hen's nest. I began to feel that I was different. Was I not already the friend of the soldiers of Lerma? And, moreover, in Mérida we were so poor that we didn't eat at a table but on a wooden wash tub—the kind used in the tropics for washing clothes—turned upside down on two large boxes, and we slept on palm mats laid on the floor. When we began to sleep in hammocks again we felt ourselves to be in the lap of luxury.

One day I told my little cousins about my friendship with the soldiers of Lerma—and how they had always told me that we are all equal—and they answered me with a terrible phrase: "We're all made from the same clay, but a chamber pot is not a pitcher."

With which my little cousins wished to indicate quite simply that they were the recipients of milk and honey from Hymettus, and the soldiers and I of less delicious and less aròmatic things. Was I not already the friend of the soldiers of Lerma? My cousins felt that I was and I thought so too, a little.

But I was never at a loss for a reply. My father had taught me the verses of the Colombian poet Santiago Pérez, and I had learned them very well, thinking of my carpenter grandfather who, like coal, had had a humble beginning:

> Said the pearl to the diamond:
> "I'm worth more than you:
> You were born from black coal,
> I from the sea's blue."
>
> And the diamond replied:
> "Your value is scant:
> You'll always be white.
> I was once black and now I give light."

My cousins laughed at such a complicated reply, but the boy, to hurt me, deliberately adjusted his necktie to impress me with his elegance in dress. I wore blouses and in the house went about in an undershirt. On holidays my mother had me wear a long denim Philippine jacket, closed up to the neck. My Mérida cousins said that I looked like a noodle.

My amusements were to play with my Carpio cousins who lived near me, or engage in rock fights with the Alpuches, boys whose patio was adjacent to mine. Also I enjoyed seeing and listening to the half-breed men and women. Although the populace is so designated in Yucatán, as a matter of fact they are actually less cross-bred and of purer Mayan extraction than the upper and middle classes. The men and women always dress in white, the latter in a linen smock or wrapper, the former in trousers and a cotton shirt—everything quite starched. They are the cleanest people in the world. They bathe as much as the Tabascans but, in addition, change their clothes every day. My father used to say that to put on their trousers, the men got up on a table and then jumped down so as to fall threaded in them as it were. Only thus could one explain that they never showed a wrinkle. The women were stunning. It was there that the Spanish novelist Valle-Inclán saw in a hotel the girl whom later he would imagine to be his paramour in the fantastic and marvelous *Summer Sonata*. The opposite happened to me, since the woman with whom I fell in love as a child was an arrogant Spanish lady who lived next to my house, and who greeted us every day saying *bona nit* (good evening). She was a Catalan.

By this time the Revolution had reachel Yucatán. Henequen, a fiber widely used in industry and the basis of the country's prosperity, had always been exported in large quantities to both Europe and the United States. The chaotic conditions of the time made this no longer possible; as a result my Yucatán cousins were also going to be impoverished and humbled.

Our childhood evolved between shootings and accounts of them. We heard that General Salvador Alvarado had hung a number of students from the trees on Montejo Boulevard; that the mother of one of them had sworn to kill him; that she in fact tried to do so, but at the last minute her pistol jammed; that they caught her and that Alvarado pardoned her. One day when my father went out to the street a heavy firing began; he returned when the hail of bullets had ceased. He was obliged to jump over dead bodies and pools of blood. He was stopped several times by men carrying pistols. This violence was a part of the rebellion of Benjamín Argumedo against the Governor, don Toribio de los Santos.

We left Mérida and the port of Campeche to return to

Términos Lagoon, but this time under different circumstances. My father had been named administrator of a firm in bankruptcy and a teacher at the *lycée*. I entered the elementary school and made up the time I had lost. This was an official school, run by the revolutionary government, but one in which the director, a distinguished and respected old man with a goatee, still perpetuated the ancient custom of beating the children with a horse whip. He used a procedure that was new to me: he would order to his room the pupils he had singled out for punishment, make them straddle one of the fifth- or sixth-grade students and, stretching their short pants tight over their buttocks, give it to them good. The horse had to be able to support the mounted rider or he got it too. One day, when I had had a fist fight, the director summoned me, but I didn't go. On another occasion when I had thrown stones at a drayman, he came personally to my room to look for me; but I took off on a rapid flight that ended at my house. My father scolded me but went with me to the school to plead my case and to beg them not to beat me then or ever.

My surroundings had changed. For a long time I had been living far from my relatives. Some were in Tabasco, and I saw those who were in Laguna only infrequently. My best friend was a classmate, Pérez, a street vendor of sweets and fruits. As a part of our games we children played Revolution, and I was in charge of delivering speeches from the benches in the patio, where I repeated only what I had overheard in the street gatherings. I always ended my discourse with our classic and ridiculous phrase "I have said." My political oratory earned me the hatred of a boy very good with his fists. He was the man of action who scorned the intellect. I proceeded to get myself some brass knuckles and from that moment decided to face men of action on their own terms.

During that period we used to go to the beach early in the morning in a cart belonging to a drayman, a friend and namesake of my father. The women undressed inside a beached boat. My mother, my sisters, and their friends bathed in chemises and drawers—in some truly abominable getups. Morals clearly dictated bathing suits. My father and I would fish in a small stream that emptied there and then, fleeing the sun and the buzzing horseflies, hurl ourselves into the water. On one occasion we realized that a shark was circling us, and it is no exaggeration to say that in the Gulf of Mexico every bather is a hero who risks his life.

It was during this time that Dr. Jordán, an intimate family friend, had died. My sisters and a cousin of mine thought they saw his ghost peeking through the window. My half-zany uncle had frightened them: during the wake he had gone about armed with a coffeepot filled with hot water, looking behind the chairs for the male *tuncuruxú*, an imaginary animal (possibly a part of Mayan tradition) that was supposed to wander about the world committing fiendish acts. The women were undressing when the "ghost," a North American Peeping Tom, moved the curtains. I, less credulous, went and advised my father, who was asleep in his hammock. He got up and, slipping along the walls, opened the street door and jumped toward the window. This was the only time I ever saw my father in an angry fight. His indignation was stronger than the alcohol of the lascivious North American, because he nailed him to the wall with a single blow. A Spanish neighbor got out of bed and tried to placate my father. It was a very droll scene because they had both been sleeping in underdrawers, those nineteenth-century ones tied at the ankles. Could there have been patriotic retaliation in my father's blows? Because some days before, on the way to swim, a friend we met told him that in Veracruz, then held by the Yankees, Mexicans were being treated with absolute scorn.

You see, my father, in his great political scepticism, did not agree with an uncle of mine, the most racist of them all, who averred in his counterrevolutionary fury, "I prefer to be kicked by a white man than by an Indian."

A short while later, we all left for Tabasco, except my father, who remained in Laguna.

7

Tabasco Recovered

My mother, very worn out during this whole period of hunger-ridden tourism—since she had been cook, laundress, chambermaid, and mother at the same time—quickly regained her strength once we arrived at San Juan Bautista. It was the end of our flight and the return to the home nest.

The place was no longer called San Juan Bautista. General Francisco J. Mújica, the revolutionary governor, had restored its ancient and beautiful name: Villahermosa.

We went to live in the house of my cousins the Martínezes. My oldest cousin, Juan, was one of the principal victims of the current situation. Born and reared in the Díaz period, a son of one of the most influential politicians of the province, his world fell apart with the collapse of the dictatorship and, especially, with the death of his father. He was reproached incessantly by teachers and classmates, who exulted particularly in cruelty to him, more than to the sons of traditionally reactionary individuals, men with a history of mistreatment of the workers, because his father's power had only recently been eclipsed, and feelings of hatred against him were still very much alive.

In the scorching sun and torrid temperature, black clothing is a blasphemy against nature; but my family loved mourning; it was spiritualistic and felt itself to be in constant communication with the dead. As a result, my aunt Cristina, as I have related before, secluded herself for several months in her room, grieving for her dead husband; so, also, the adolescence of my sisters and girl cousins was saddened by their mourning garb. My cousin Juan wore a black suit that the tropical sun turned green. It was the materialization of his wrath and grief over the treacherous assassination of his father, and the indiscreet and sadistic happiness of those who hated him.

My oldest cousin indeed lived all the drama of the thwarted counterrevolution. Was he a reactionary? At his age he could scarcely be called one, and even less in an atmosphere where the terms "reaction" and "revolution" were losing their true meanings, and had become so elastic that at either extreme they were now highly ambiguous. The social vicissitudes of his time had placed him, as they had all the Foucher clan, in a difficult and equivocal position, inclined toward counterrevolution. The angle in his case was even more acute.

I missed the ideological preparation for the Revolution. I was caught up in the moment of struggle but was not a participant in the planning. When I reached the age of reason, I found myself in a world of war and killing. Boys from rich and reactionary families would disappear one day from their classrooms and their homes: they had gone to swell the ranks of Ramón Ramos, Manuel Ferrer Vega, Fernando Villar, or any other Carranza or anti-Carranza leader, more as an outlet for their youthful violence and as a mandate from the violent history of the Tabascan, than as a result of deeply held political convictions. All I could see was that people were killing one another, many without knowing just why. But, if we leave out of account the inherited mandate to rule of some and the inflamed political passions of others, the peasants of Tabasco, those who sacked my house in 1914 and those condemned to the wages of want and to the pillory, these peasants did indeed know why they were fighting. But they had by now reverted to silence and, isolated in the far-away province, distant from Zapatist hopes and the avenging fury of Francisco Villa, they continued to suffer under a relentless injustice.

My cousin was the son, on one side of the family, of a brave man who had been powerful during the dictatorship; on the other he was the son of a woman with very clear ideas about social justice and truly Christian principles, which she practiced as passionately as unobtrusively in her daily life. Moreover, my cousin knew himself to be the grandson of an honorable, selfless man, lavishly endowed with the riches of heaven and earth: of don Manuel Foucher, in whom politics and poetry were but an outward manifestation of his abundant love for the people. He had, then, been born into an artistocratic family of exalted position, with a well-marked history of leadership. In the Tabascan milieu, so fraught with violent passions, he was the son of a man who had commanded. He was one of those who enjoyed abundance while many lacked the bare necessities. He doubtless thought that what he had was his and his alone. I too thought this. However, it was my luck that while I believed in private property, I had none. My father was not rich nor had he been powerful. On that account the rebels, except for the most inflamed ones—like my fifth-year teacher—never attacked his name.

My cousin could not have deliberately chosen to be a reactionary. However, his ancestry, distinguished by aristocratic respectability and a land-owning tradition; his deep-seated enmity toward those who had assassinated, or now took pleasure in the assassination of, his father; as well as the atmosphere of primitive, exaggerated virility and barbarous vengeance of the province, impelled him toward a militant position in the camp of the Revolution's enemies. On the other hand the maternal tradition, ever-present as a mute criticism of the complacent happiness and smug self-satisfaction of the privileged clan was, at the same time, the basis for a silent understanding of the popular cause and for possible dedication to its defense.

My cousin knew how to break horses and swim the great rivers; he could handle weapons. He felt himself to be marked for great things, and he visualized himself, from his exalted position, as a dispenser of justice. His youthful ambitions were lofty but not unwholesome. They were generous plans derived in a spirit of tropically vital and impetuous individualism.

The shift in his political position from left to right could well have been accelerated by the blind and unbridled hatred of the fools and the venom of certain false leaders of the people. I well recall the day when Benjamín, the village barber, while shaving him, wounded him treacherously with a wall-clock pendulum, opening a great gash in his forehead. My cousin—young, strong Tabascan that he was—seized the barber by the scruff of the neck and the seat of his pants, dragged him into the street, and beat his head against the streetcar rails until people pulled him from his hands. Only my cousin's bravery and defiance saved him from a lynching. There was an uproar in Villahermosa, fierce glances at my aunt's house and its surveillance by Chico Ratón, one of the most impassioned revolutionary leaders of the town. Fortunately my aunt Cristina, rising above the hatreds of the street and the adolescent violence of her sons and nephews, showed everyone, through her dispassionate neutrality that a person was not guilty for having inherited wealth, a thirst for command, and political leadership; nor, by the same token, were those guilty who felt unremitting hunger being transformed into a commensurate thirst for vengeance.

We went to live on another hill, that of Esquipulas. For a boy, living on a hill is a delight: enormous walls on one side, covered with climbing plants and small insects; on the other, tempting rooftops within easy reach. At that time I was studying national history. This was the first truly impassioned intellectual interest of my life. Every day my cousin Panchito Carpio and I climbed to the roof of a small, nearby house. There I read or related to him the torture of Cuauhtémoc, the last Aztec emperor who fought against the Spaniards. It was the one page of history that most enraptured me. And then there was the account of the execution of José María Morelos, great figure of Mexican independence, in San Cristóbal Ecatepec. I recall that the school text, by Torres Quintero, said that the waters of the lake had swollen and lovingly absorbed the shed blood. The passage ended on an emphatic note: "There was the hand of God." Naïve as I was about supernatural matters, I looked for a hand in the picture, not comprehending that the rising waters were a divine intervention, part of the hidden designs of Providence.

The elementary school made chauvinists of us. We hated the Spaniards as Spaniards, and reserved a special loathing for Pedro de Alvarado, the perpetrator of the cruel Indian massacres; we adored Cuauhtémoc, who defended the great Tenochtitlán (Mexico City) and who, when forced to surrender to Cortés, asked the latter to kill him with his own dagger; and Cacamatzin, who stoned countless Spaniards to death. We blushed with repugnance at the very mention of Montezuma, the Aztec emperor who surrendered Mexico City to the Spaniards; of Malinche, the concubine of Cortés; of the treacherous Indians who supported Cortés against the Aztecs and so betrayed their country. We were at once indignant and distressed by the intelligence and audacity of Hernán Cortés. Our reading of Torres Quintero's book was an impassioned one, and it was almost too much for us when our teacher said, "There were fewer of them and they were evil, but they had horses and harquebuses and so defeated our ancestors."

The three centuries of the colonial period weighed heavily on our souls. We passed hastily over the worthy missionaries Bartolomé de las Casas, Motolinia, Sahagún, and Vasco de Quiroga, and the good viceroys Revillagigedo and Bucareli. The "good guys" interested neither our teacher nor us. Their names might somehow dampen our jingoistic fury: it was best to give them the back of our hand. And our jubilation knew no bounds when we approached the period of Independence. We wept over the death of Fray Melchor de Talamantes and the assassination of Licentiate Verdad—the two precursors of Mexican independence—but then we would mutter, in a happy rage, "Now for sure those damned Spaniards will get what's what . . ."

We laughed with glee on seeing the popular hero Pípila burning the door of the Spanish stronghold, or the valiant patriot Hermenegildo Galeana laughingly defying the bullets at the siege of Cuautla. In our eyes, Calleja, the general of the Spanish forces, was as vile as the conquistadors. We called Hidalgo, the father of Mexican independence, "the venerable old man of Dolores," after the village where the struggle for independence began. Morelos, the other great initiator of independence, was the gleaming sword that filled us with the greatest enthusiasm, and his execution heightened our hatreds. Quintana Roo and Dr. Cos, the ideologists of the independence movement, were the most cultured men on the whole planet.

"The damned Spaniards never had anyone as valiant and cultured as our heroes."—hatred for the despicable Spaniards as Spaniards, love for the Mexicans as Mexicans; happiness over the slaughter of Spaniards, sadness over the death of our patriots; an unreasoning zeal very similar to religious fanaticism: passion, bloodshed, and fire to nourish our fantasies.

When we read, on one page that must have escaped chauvinistic censorship, how General Nicolás Bravo, after learning that his father had been shot by royalist troops, freed three hundred Spanish prisoners, we cried in unison, "But how stupid, how very stupid of don Nicolás. He did that because he was a Mexican. The cursed Spaniards pardon no one."

No voice was raised to point out to us that there were *mestizos*, and even Indians, who were cruel and overbearing to their workers, and as deserving of our opprobrium as were the men who had been born in Spain, the country of our conquerors, and later prospered in Mexico. We could never imagine that men were exploited in Spain: that was a country where there were only executioners and aristocrats, who came to America to enslave and to seek gold, and to rob with their scales as their forbears had robbed with their swords.

The atmosphere of our society supported our error. The Spanish colony was considered the richest, the most aristocratic of Tabasco. Prejudice, the legacy of centuries of subjugation by Spain, had conferred a high rank on those who in many cases had come from a humble social condition in their country only to deny it, forget it, and betray it in America. They too had learned from childhood to believe in the theory of racial supremacy and to scorn the conquered Indian. Surely their village priest had not pointed out to them that the saying "to play the Indian," meaning "to pass for an idiot," had its origin in an imperialistic Spanish past. They came to America to take full advantage of the implications of the saying and to grasp everything in sight.

The very chauvinists and radicals of my province were, beneath their hatred, secretly envious of the whiteness and the grace of the Spaniards. In my home, a young Spaniard from the borders of Bilbao, one Pepe Samaniego, was admired more than anyone.

"I'll have me money, a lotta money," was his constant remark.

He was esteemed much more than Dr. Filipo Martínez, a

studious, cultured, but very Indian physician who was a rival of the Spaniard Samaniego in the courtship of one of my sisters.

The best friend of the family was a big hulk of a Majorcan Spaniard, who was making much money in his grocery store, and who was so strong he could lift a table with his teeth. That Hercules was the only one allowed to employ coarse, embarrassing interjections in my house. Any Tabascan suitor, rich, handsome, or brave as he may have been, was in jeopardy if a Spanish grocer set his sights on his intended. The Spaniard won out, although he may have made, or have been making, his fortune as an overseer of one of the chicle plantations, notorious for their abominable working conditions, or as the proprietor of a cantina. The family would reason, "He's aristocratic, say what they will."

The Spaniards, good or bad, had carte blanche. Mexico continued to be, in spite of the anti-Spanish primary education, a conquered land. The memory of three centuries gave the Spanish an aura of aristocracy, although under one's breath he might call them "Spaniards smuggled in in barrels," as many of them had been in earlier periods.

None of the immigrants could compete with them. The Turks—as the Arabs, Syro-Lebanese, and authentic Turks were called—were thoroughly scorned. Accept a Syro-Lebanese or his son in the Casino? Only white Tabascans and Spaniards went there (or half-breeds and Indians, if rich: money had a way of making one forget the color of the skin); but a Turk? Impossible! It was for this reason that my uncle's love affair was so socially repugnant.

"There comes the Turkish girl," and my sister and I would cross to the other side of the street.

"To think of it, involved with a Turkish girl," my aunts would exclaim with a grimace of nausea.

But it is, of course, undeniable that the Spaniards had a remarkable capacity for adaptation. They had finally learned to take a daily bath, they dressed in denim or Palm Beach, and even affected a provincial accent.

Except that when bananas began to be sold to the Yankees, and the latter started to get the scent of Tabascan oil, Spanish bonds began to drop in price. The gringos were the new conquistadors: as technicians in the electric companies, as engineers with the oil concerns, as partners of the new bosses. The beautiful Spanish race was not physically superior to these husky, blue-eyed boys who played baseball, taught tennis to the young ladies of Villahermosa, swam like fish, and danced an excellent fox trot.

But the blue-eyed ones were leaving and the Spaniards remained: Asturians and Majorcans, obdurate and unyielding, but by now fathers of Mexican children.

One day when I was discussing these questions with my cousin Panchito in our splendid watchtower that faced on a modest little street, we were moved to hasty flight by the voice of an old mustachioed demagogue who was rebuking us from the door of his house: "These are no longer the days of don Porfirio, you suckers."

In the revolutionary fury of those times there were fanatics who, despite our ingenuous ten years, harassed us as though we were conspirators. Not only did my parents, with their memories of past family greatness, try to make me a counter-revolutionary, but I was so inclined also by the attacks of the ignorant and the violent, incomprehensible to my childish understanding. Thus they, in effect, kept strengthening my innate esteem for don Porfirio. But these gutter insults didn't really matter: it was in the school where they were going to make me feel like a bourgeois child and clinch, with their offenses and scorn, my admiration for the bemedaled chest of General Díaz.

I learned many things during my life in the house on the hill. I spent my days in the patio picking at flowers and fruit, examining and torturing the endless varieties of tropical insects.

It was a very large patio, a sort of abandoned orchard or garden, an ideal spot in which childish fantasy could fashion a thousand legends. But it was not legend but a real occurrence, and a most grievous one, that I recall: one day my chicken, my very favorite chicken, drowned in the deep well of the patio, and before my terrified eyes.

My day-to-day observation of these domestic birds was much less tragic. Since my days in Campeche I had been disturbed by the relationship of cocks and hens. While living there I had asked my father why the roosters danced about the hens, and why later their eyes shone and their crests turned scarlet. Despite his great erudition, he never gave me a satisfactory explanation; but neither did he confound me with lies. I have the feeling that he really wished to satisfy my curiosity but didn't know exactly how to do it. But one thing is certain, the cocks and hens of Campeche and Tabasco taught me the mechanics of male and female copulation. A male cousin of my own age finally removed all my remaining doubts.

One day we were playing camp in the Plazuela del Aguila. This is a war game. The boys, divided into two groups, start individual contests, until one overcomes his adversary and drags him prisoner to his camp. The number of prisoners determines the victory. Physically I was very weak and rickety, and therefore I was always one of the first to be taken prisoner. Once overcome, I would watch the game or perhaps go to the house of some of my cousins. That day I did the latter, and learned that another little cousin had been born. My aunt, naturally, was in bed. I went in to see her and she showed me the baby, which looked horrible to me, as have all recently born babies since then. It looked like nothing so much as a wet puppy.

I left the house with the same old, disturbing rumbling in my head: how had it been born? Someone had revealed to my contemporary how children were "ordered." I knew they were born of the mother, but about the "order," the way in which they were "ordered"—despite my knowing the secret of the cock and the hen—my doubts were enormous. My young cousin took me aside to let me in on the secret and said to me: "Well, the man does this and the woman that, and then at nine months . . ." He was younger than I but had older brothers, while I lived tied to the apron strings of my sisters. With some pretext or another I withdrew; with no pretext at all I set out running. I continued to run, taking a shortcut through various small streets, avoiding people, until I reached my house, flushed, panting, and distressed. My mother observed me and remarked, "Something is the matter with this boy." I don't know what had happened to me, why it upset me so to learn about the mechanics of life.

In the house on Esquipulas Hill I was the witness to a number of tragic spectacles. This was the road to the cemetery, and the executions were carried out there. One day a hair-raising entourage passed by my house: they were taking a man to be shot and many of the curious were following the platoon, among them boys from my school. I didn't have the courage to accompany them. During my stay in Campeche, they had become accustomed to witnessing shootings, or at least boasted that they had.

And so my tormented and revolutionary childhood unfolded amidst sexual perplexities and hard human truths.

On the brighter side I have one very amusing recollection. In front of my house there lived an old bricklayer who had become wealthy from some treasures of the colonial period he had discovered while razing a thick wall. I can't forget don Tino, seated in front of his house, getting some fresh air. He had made an effort to improve himself, had learned to read, and always sat with a large book on his knees. It was a copy of *Mexico Across the Centuries;* but he always said, without realizing that he was being ridiculous, that he was reading *Mexico Crossed by the Centuries.* He also said some very amusing things about the women who lived around the corner, whom he called the "prostiputes."

Near my house was the Instituto Juárez, where my cousin studied. And in the side alley, in the classical little side street, the brothel of Chepa Chorizo. I was disturbed equally by the house of knowledge and by the house of vice. I entered the first on one occasion and dreamed of one day being as wise as the youths who had taken me there. I looked with veneration at maps, spheres, apparatus for physics experiments, and an idol that was standing in the vestibule; and I was charmed by the patio, shaded by magnificent examples of the great breadfruit tree. In that school, under those trees, among those mysterious machines, I knew that my father had passed his youth as a poor student. As for Chepa Chorizo's house, I never had the courage to enter it, although when I passed by, the pitiful women would beckon to me with hisses, greatly disturbing my tender young ears.

8

My Father

One day we received word that my father was arriving from Laguna, and we made preparations at once to move into a larger house. It was then, for the first time, that I took a really scrutinizing look at him.

He was of medium stature, very strong and stocky. When he was in a mesh undershirt, I liked to measure his remarkably muscular arms. They had told me he could deliver a tremendous blow, harder than anyone. In some sort of gymnastic contest he beat ten of my uncles. He was dark-complexioned, very sunburned, slightly yellowish, with the sickly pallor of the tropics. His head was very wide and he had an ample forehead marked by two deep bald spots. We children, who were studying geography, called the strip of hair lying between them "the peninsula." The peninsula, we used to say, then became an island: at its base a small spot of sparse hair developed later on. His eyes were very, very bright and when speaking they became animated or, at times, sweet and wistful. When he became angry they gave off sparks, but this was only a brief flash. His friends avoided such flashes of anger by agreeing with him or by remaining silent, and my mother by touching his foot underneath the table. Sometimes this tactic didn't work out but, rather, produced the opposite effect. Then he would scold her, saying, "Why are you touching my foot?" But his friends were able to get all the help they wanted from him. And that was not all: he was so indulgent by nature that they were able to lie to him, to rob him, to reduce his share of profit in an enterprise with his full knowledge. When people told him something pitiful, sad, or tragic his eyes would fill with tears. He would take out his handkerchief to dry them and would say, "That's enough. Let's not talk about it any more."

My father had a large, thick, slightly graying mustache, but fortunately he kept it stylishly trimmed. It annoyed us when the spaghetti got entangled in it, and this was frequently, despite the fact that, with a gesture very much his own, he would brush it back to each side in two bunches before eating. He had a heavy beard and he shaved twice a day, once in the morning and again at night. What most interested us about his face was a little hole, a small indentation exactly in the middle of the right cheek, and we enjoyed playing with that so very smooth skin. We had the history of this scar at our fingertips, and recounted it whenever we spoke of adventures in which one risks his life: a poisonous, green fly had bitten him when he was a child. They made an incision and cauterized the wound, but the little hole remained. To be truthful, however, I don't know whether he told us this or whether we made it up. His hair was very fine and curly, much like Negroes' hair, although not precisely. The barbers cut it short and this was very becoming to him. When we insisted, he used to put pomade on his hair and it shone marvelously. We always liked our father a great deal and thought him most charming. I don't honestly feel that this judgment is a biased one, because years later I learned that more than one lady shared our opinion of him with perhaps excessive enthusiasm.

All of his person gave an impression of strength and joviality. He was a spontaneous and joyful conversationalist. He played every manner of game with us: ball, marbles, jacks, bullfighting, and kite flying. Together we swam in the sea of Campeche, and on the beach he played as many pranks as I. Naturally I always used the familiar, second person form of the verb in addressing him, and he frequently spoke to me employing an affectionate diminutive of my name. But make no mistake about it, this was not familiarity at the price of respect! My father knew many things, and this impressed us tremendously. Everyone went to him for advice or to ask him to counsel their sons. The young leaders of the Revolution were always coming to the house to consult with him about different matters. How then could *we* argue with him? He was also very good to the poor, and was in every way most honorable. So how could we treat *him* badly? And, besides, he had a violent temper and we didn't like to see his eyes flash. It was enough to hear him shout for silence, for the quarrels of my sisters, among themselves or with me, to end immediately. He had no need to strike or punish us. In our house there was a great discipline, springing from a tacit understanding between children and parents. The fears and hardships endured during the Revolution had bound us very closely together. We were more studious, more reflective, more serious than normal. Ours were childish lives absorbed by a tremendous spectacle. As a result we never strayed from the straight road. Of course it must be said that the road was an ample and commodious one: we studied as and when we wished, or at least our parents were able to make us think that's the way it was.

My father had a habit, viewed very dourly by certain of his relatives, of calling things by their right names, of calling a spade a spade. He was characterized by a naturalness and a spontaneity that I have later discovered to be Spanish in nature, or at least resembled very closely the ingenuousness and spontaneity of the Spaniards. On the high plateau of Mexico City there is a tendency toward the understatement, the euphemism, excellent to be sure under certain conditions, very bad in others. There are certain words that "respectable people" can't use either in public or in intimate circumstances. To refer, for example, to the buttocks, or to physiological functions, we Mexicans have recourse to circumlocutions and subterfuges. I don't know whether it is also possibly a result of our education that the classical "son of a bitch" has been changed to a milder, more euphemistic expression, although this and similar ones now come across about as strongly as the originals. As I have said, my father always called a spade a spade with complete frankness, and at times made use of very Spanish interjections. He was the incarnation of naturalness: uncomplicated, without subterfuge. I believe it was on this account that he got along so well with the soldiers of the Revolution, although he had not fought with them, and with the people, who considered him one of their own.

This plain, outspoken manner did not prevent his being marked by an exquisite, authentic sensitivity. He had, in generous measure, that Mexican courtesy, an amalgam of Spanish nobility and native gentleness, so superior to British aloofness, French unctuousness, or the fawning flattery of the Italians. And in my father's case it was richly imbued with tropical warmth and virile self-assurance. One of his pupils, Francisco J. Santamaría, said of him as a teacher that he recognized "the gentle secret of the French writer Rabelais: sweet severity," and that "he was the personification of smiling austerity, in whose scowling frown, as on the surface of a serene but imposing sea, were to be read all the emotions of his soul, and all the energy of his character. He was a man of violent impetuousness; but he was so perfectly educated that gentility and the most exquisite amiability adorned his person as they might a lady's."

He was as unpretentious in his dress as in his conduct. He never aspired to be stylish, nor could he have been. With the physical force that was his, there was no cloth that wouldn't have wrinkled on his frame. To avoid this one needs a less vigorous nature, less energetic movements. In the tropics he always used his Panama hat. He would put this on very carefully and properly in the house, in my mother's presence, but once in the street, for greater comfort, he used to push it up with the back of his hand as far as the nape of his neck, exposing his handsome forehead. Standing in the doorway of my house on Encarnación Hill, I can see him approaching, my sisters and I running to greet him with kisses. In Mexico City he always wore his black felt hat and fine, but not too fancy, suits. He liked comfort, and, as a convenience, although it was not stylish to do so, he wore neckties with a pretied knot, held in place with a small wire contrivance that hooked onto his gold collar button. And, although a magistrate, he was one of the first to use shirts with a soft, attached collar, without starch, like his soul. He wore, as a further convenience, elastic military boots, to save himself the bother of continually fastening.

What a noble, generous, and upright type he was, so frank and open! In his Tabascan surroundings he didn't pretend to be wise, pure white, a founding father, not even brave. Not even brave! This was the nth degree of unpretentiousness in Tabasco. When it was necessary he could be calm and energetic; but my father did not have a propensity toward bravery, common to both sides of my Tabascan family. His was perhaps a superior valor: that of daring to be a smiling, amiable, and cordial man in a world and period of unbridled violence.

As for his tastes in reading, my father knew the Spanish classics and the realistic novelists: Galdós, Pereda, Valera. From among French writers he read Victor Hugo, Zola, Daudet, and, naturally, the Encyclopedists. But prose was not his favorite literary form. His feelings—trammeled by the considerations and findings of his tribunal—were inclined rather toward poetry, and the works of the Spanish-American poets Rubén Darío, Gutiérrez Nájera, Amado Nervo, and González Martínez were familiar to me from childhood. One of the most painful and disturbing misfortunes to befall me as a child was to have accidentally spilled an inkwell on *The Death of the Swan* by González Martínez. I was unable to find another copy with which to replace it, although I looked all over Laguna: first in the bookstores and then among devotees of literature. I finally had to tell my father. I imposed my own punishment by refusing on the following Sunday to accept the *peso* given me every week to go to a dilapidated theater they called a movie house, and by idly passing the time with my grief—which came from having aggrieved him—playing on the lumber floats tied on the beach, a dangerous pastime, resolutely prohibited by my parents. My sisters and I copied verses by these and other poets in a book dedicated to the Muses. It contained some things in very bad taste, even poetry of such second-rate writers as Blanco Belmonte and Narciso Díaz de Escovar.

My mother's family was exceedingly romantic—this a legacy from my grandfather Foucher. We knew some of his verses from memory, not always the best, in which one can detect traces of the Spanish romantic poets Espronceda and Zorrilla, and of the Cuban poet Heredia. All are valuable, even the most carelessly written, because of the nobility and ingenuousness they reflect.

Unfortunately my father never had any free time, and I can't recall that he ever took a vacation. He knew French very well and loved Spanish literature especially, although he never attained what could be called a scholarly knowledge of the latter.

What I recall with most pleasure are fragments of the songs he sang, almost all of them sportively humorous. I wish I remembered them all because they were much better than the verses he recited.

I don't recall ever having heard my father sing seriously. He always sang at home, but in fun. Half jokingly he would dance a clog in the folk dances of Laguna and, later on, when he used to escort my sisters to the Christmas parties and festivities, he would dance the Mexican Hat Dance and even the Aragonese *jota* with them. He was a complex personality: energetic and gentle, serious and gay.

My mother was of another stripe. Silent, timid, a little sad, self-centered, although a great conversationalist in private, she couldn't keep pace with that buoyant life. This was the only lamentable thing in my household: the temperamental differences between my parents. My mother was extremely conscientious, very intelligent, and possessed perhaps a greater sensitivity and a keener sense of humor than my father, but she was a spirit in repose, not geared for action, preferring observation to movement. She worshipped my father, but there was somehow a great sadness in that love that my childish mind could not define. I heard her sighs and observed her silence, but I couldn't fathom them. The expression on her face became, in an old age buffeted by life and the dramatic deaths of children or nephews, one of resigned bitterness as a constant state of mind short of complete dejection, one of anguish held in check by the stoic tradition of the Mexican, and borne with fatalistic forbearance.

"Patience, patience," she would say, leaning forward with a gesture or resignation until her chin rested in her open palm.

I observed her thus on the death of her daughter and of her husband, and when other dear ones met death, tragedy, or slander.

My father had adapted to the discipline of his marriage. He was never away from home at night, he was never late, and he took no mysterious trips. But my mother was highly intuitive, and she declared that she was more fearful of the "dayscapades" than of the "nightscapades." A few legends of this sort were hatched about him, perhaps with some foundation. This made for a certain unhappiness in our home, as it does in all households, despite the abundant virtues of my parents. Those annoyances cloaked in silence—my mother employed the great tactic of not speaking—hurt us children greatly.

We always sided with our mother, although neither of them ever said a word to us about their differences, and in so doing we were rising in protest against the double standard. And this was the only thing that at times disturbed my intimate relationship with my father. He made my mother, so completely and selflessly devoted to him and to us, suffer, and I harbored, deep down in my being, a strange resentment toward him. This was a resentment that wished to disappear but never did.

9

Politics and the Tropics

During the time we occupied the house on Madero Avenue, I lived intensely and came close to participating in the political struggle.

This was in 1918, and by now the Revolution had been torn apart by internal dissent. Since 1915 Carranza and Villa had been at one another's throats, and while Tabasco remained loyal to Carranza, there was discord. The years of the Revolution in Tabasco were years of inflamed passions; those both of the rebel leaders and of many of the reactionaries had managed to distort the Revolution's aims and character.

There were two candidates for governor of my province: don Carlos Greene, the leader of the red, or revolutionary (radical) party, and don Luis Felipe Domínguez, that of the blue, counterrevolutionary (conservative) party. I don't know whether the followers of don Carlos displayed the red symbol intentionally and with a knowledge of its historical significance, or whether this was merely a coincidence, easily explained by the penchant of popular taste toward this lively and vital color; in any event the reds were the radicals, the revolutionists. As a result General Greene drew more adherents from among the people, while don Luis Felipe found his support in the middle class and the wealthy. For example, my mother's family, including my sisters, were blues. One of my female relatives wore both the blue bow and the picture of Félix Díaz, the nephew of don Porfirio, who failed as a soldier, as a politician, and even as an exile, because no one in Mexico ever knew —or cared—when he ceased to be one. Another relative wore blue blouses and red shoes in order to continually trample the symbol of the enemy group. I was neither one nor the other, or I was both. On some days I was blue and on others red; but more often I was blue. This was another period of complexities: on the one hand I was impressed by the fact that my parents and their most intimate friends, that is to say, the "aristocratic" people of Tabasco, were members of the blue party; but on the other hand I was confounded by the fact that in meetings those same people also spoke in the name of, and in support of, the Revolution. By now they were using the word Revolution, without meaning, just as the Spanish monarchists would speak, opportunistically, after its downfall, in the name of the Republic. On the other hand I was very much affected by the fact that two of my father's favorite pupils, the orator Martínez de Escobar and the distinguished philologist Santamaría, were reds: the first, who wore an unforgettable checked suit and literally worked himself into a sweaty lather with his booming voice and his impetuous, interminable "resistance" oratory; and Pancho Santamaría, thin of body with eyes like those of a lynx, who threw a hypnotic spell over me in the

meetings. A classmate took me one day to the Greene head-
quarters, and tried to make me kneel before the picture of don
Carlos, draped with red banners and bouquets of carnations.
People thought me a blue. The fact of the matter is I was
carrying water on both shoulders. I remember my surprise
upon finding out that my cousin Pánfilo, the owner of the
millinery store whom I, like a good Tabascan boy, admired
because he was brave and would stand up to anyone, belonged
to the blue party. How could this be if he were poor, a crafts-
man, if he worked with his hands? But then the case of the
Pombo family, of my uncles Casiano and Pablo Pombo, made
the situation somewhat clearer to me. The one, a peaceful
landowner, was a blue; the other, poor, and a passionate revolutionary, was a red.

But my intuitions were unable to crystallize in an atmosphere of political confusion that tended to falsify everything.
Why was it that among the reds there were also ranchers,
landowners, and bosses who had used the pillory and the whip
against the rural peon? I was fully aware of the reputations of
certain old men of the revolutionary party as executioners and
abusive overseers. And why, if they professed to be for the
people, did they stay so wealthy? I suspected that it was because they were frauds, that they had eased themselves into the
ranks of the Revolution in order to corrupt and betray its aims.
And how could don Carlos Greene accept them and at the
same time attack and vilify my conservative relatives as rich
exploiters? Because, according to my family, he needed the
money of his affluent supporters for propaganda. But what
were these people going to demand of him later? How could
he be against them tomorrow if they had supported him in the
past? And, if he were able to wriggle out of his commitments,
wouldn't this portend a lessening of his power, since it would
mean the loss of their support?

Under such circumstances, who were the bad and who the
good? Such reflections left me little choice in making up my

mind, and hid the truth from me, the search for which was going to torment my ingenuous liberal adolescence.

My father had another pupil, Dimas Gamarra, who used to come to visit him sometimes. He was from a rich, land-owning family which, as such, enjoyed a very bad reputation. But even so he was a violent radical and people had nicknamed him the "Red." His uncle, don Manuel, an intimate friend of my father and who, while we were wandering through Campeche and Yucatán in dire straits, had loaned us money, was also a revolutionary. I recall that Dimas, at the band concerts in Juárez Park, took it upon himself to foment the greatest possible disorder, to the great distress of the high-class young women. Every night the aristocrats of Villahermosa strolled about the statue of Juárez, set on a rubblework pedestal and bearing the inscription: "Peace is respect for the rights of others." The populace had their area marked off: they circulated *outside* the park. Imagine such a thing at the height of the Revolution! Dimas would induce the bolder working girls to mingle in the ranks of the aristocratic young ladies and would try in every conceivable way to ridicule the established hierarchy. The Little Copper Princess had a role in this. She was a stunning woman of the people, dark-complexioned, arrogant, with jet-black hair and a sensuous mouth that kindled my precocious desires. She had been so nicknamed because of her tempting cinnamon-colored skin and because of her reign over all the men. No sooner did she appear than the aristocratic young ladies fled the park with their noses in the air, amid the derisive laughter of Dimas and his companions. He was a robust hulk of a boy, with washed-out green, malevolent eyes. I knew him by sight, by name, and from a chance happening. I had a book that had been his. One day my sisters had needed a copy of the *Grammar* of the Royal Spanish Academy, and it was impossible to find one in the bookstores of Villahermosa. The "Red" loaned his copy to my father. In the book I found a series of crude expressions, doubtless written in the margins by its owner to add "charm" to the Spanish language classes. These he had constructed by linking first names with real or imaginary family names, and the combinations resulted in picturesque vulgarities. They were the worst kind of scurrilities and I have never forgotten them. I can well imagine that they were not class exercises! I laughed at them but I could not feel much congeniality toward a person who spent his time collecting such examples of dirty insolence.

However, I did have a liking for other revolutionary friends of my father, especially Santamaría and Martínez de Escobar. They wanted my father to be a red. I recall that two days before the elections they came to get him and then the three walked and talked with Greene. Doubtless my father was torn by the same perplexities as I. Or, put another way, mine were only a reflection of his. He did not have faith in the personal merits of, any of the candidates. Moreover, he saw power being contended for by "respectable people," called Dominguistas (conservatives), turned revolutionaries, and by self-proclaimed friends of the people who pinned a red bow on their chests and associated with cruel landowners whom they considered redeemed by virtue of the ribbon they too wore in their lapels. My father defended the counterrevolutionary prisoners, but he never wore a blue ribbon, never spoke ill of Greene, nor voted in the elections.

At that time the school was the rack of torment for me. I was a good student. I studied during my fourth year with María Dolores Pérez Oropeza, who was a staunch and enthusiastic revolutionary, but still not excessively dominated by political passions. Only once, in our agriculture class, when I refused to dig, she pulled my ears in a gentle, symbolic way. She obviously attributed my refusal to the affectations of an aristocratic boy who turned up his nose at manual labor. But my great misfortune was to be promoted to the fifth grade. What sorrows awaited me there! It was my just or unjust impression that my teacher was a man who substituted demagoguery for capacity. This is a not unusual way to earn one's living—excusable, I suppose, like most procedures used for such an indispensable requirement—but, for me, it was a sad business. We called him Chin Chun Chan because he looked like an Oriental. He questioned me every day on the lesson and I always answered very well. But no sooner had I sat down than he would ask, "Aren't you ashamed to have the son of a reactionary surpass you?" I came to hate him blindly and furiously. During the recess I wandered about alone, worrying, and thinking about how I could free myself of his dislike. He attributed my aloofness as a self-engrossed child to pride, to a repugnance toward playing with the children of the populace, and this he said in the middle of the class, inflaming the passions of my classmates. One day I had a dispute with another boy. On leaving the class he incited us to fight. I—although a Tabascan and accustomed to fighting—failed that day. I was afraid: afraid of Chin Chun Chan's face, of the surroundings, of everything. At that moment I was, because of my teacher, the enemy; I represented abominable reaction. He was the one most responsible for my not being a revolutionary, despite the liking I had for my revolutionary friends. But months later he left, and I had the great good fortune of acquiring a new teacher—a very pretty young woman. I saw her for the last time one day when I was picking up stones on Encarnación Hill. I saw her coming from afar, climbing the hill on Hidalgo Street. She was a tall, slender, delicate woman—her skin, the color of a pine nut; her hair, curly and black; her eyes, lively and slanting, Oriental; her mouth, plump and sensual. I was no longer attending classes, because my trip to Mexico City had been decided on. Taking leave of me, she gave me an unforgettable kiss—on the mouth!

At this time there was an unprecedented flood, affecting all the rivers of the region. Although I didn't know it then, the flood was going to be, indirectly, the reason for our later trip to the capital. It turned out that my sister's tuberculosis, for which she would eventually go to Mexico City for treatment, had been induced by the miasmas arising from the receding waters and by the ensuing pestilence.

All night the river roared in the distance. In the morning when I got out of my hammock I found the house full of water. This of course alarmed our parents, but was a source of joy for us children, especially when the water level reached a foot and a half inside the house. This meant that one could now navigate outside. We lived like this for two weeks—happy ones for me. We went barefoot and moved about in rowboats and kayaks. We traversed the town and its surroundings. The river current dragged along bodies of dogs, cats, and horses; bunches of bananas, tree trunks, and green clumps of hyacinth —a host of captivating objects and colors. I felt the tragedy of the situation only when, in the midst of the countryside, we came across a modest little house almost completely covered with water, with the family, the dogs, the cats, and the squawking chickens all on the roof. Another boat, more powerful than ours, was able to rescue them. Some of my more daring friends, who were good swimmers, plunged in and swam right in the street in front of my house, where the slope toward the river began. But our pleasure, that of children fascinated with the unexpected tropical Venice in which we found ourselves, was a thoughtless one. Actually the flood was baneful: it took riches and lives and left pestilence behind. When the waters receded, the city fell victim to its miasmas, but we children could still amuse ourselves. There were large numbers of tiny frogs, and millions of little toads that we kept squashing as we walked and that sounded like firecrackers. But we were also witnesses of the macabre: funeral processions passed by, houses emitted the nauseating odor of medicine, windows and doors remained closed and with black crepe on the frames. In Tabasco the flood was followed by Spanish influenza. In my own house my oldest sister fell ill, and that was the beginning of her slow death, of her painful extinction.

This was the period of my first reading. In this as in other matters, good and bad, I followed in the footsteps of my cousin Juan. By this time he was studying in Mexico City, but his mother allowed me to use his library. I read from cover to cover the novels of the detective Nick Carter. I was fascinated by him and his two assistants, Chick and Patsy. The result was that, with some youths in the neighborhood, Chenés and Faustino, and a few other boys, I organized a secret society. Faustino was the son of the owner of the Merino Theater and had a rubber-stamp vignette in the form of a pointing finger used in preparing the programs; we used it to stamp threatening letters that we sent to our victims. That was our symbol and from it I proposed the name of the gang: "The Pointing Hand." This was an adaption of "The Clenched Fist," the title of a very popular movie of the time. From the beginning we devoted ourselves to the persecution of our sisters' beaux; because the Tabascan boy, in keeping with the concept of honor seen in the plays of the seventeenth-century Spanish dramatist Calderón, had the clear duty to harass his potential brothers-in-law. The matter of armament was a simple one. We picked bitter oranges from the trees along the street, stored them in strategic places, and then threw them at our victims' heads. But some difficulty or another arose and I saw myself obliged, for the first time in my life, to dictate a political document: my resignation.

Then, with some other boys of a different sort, I founded a social and literary society in which, among other things, speeches of a political nature were delivered. The atmosphere of the street intoxicated us. I, naturally, constituted the opposition. My persecution at the hands of Chin Chun Chan, my parents' opinions, and overheard mutterings about the corruption of various revolutionary leaders in power at this time caused me to retreat toward an admiration for don Porfirio Díaz from which I would not deviate during the whole of my adolescence.

But the social and literary society had a worse and more Tabascan end than the "Pointing Hand." This was a shame, because the society had taught us discipline, cooperation, and thrift. We had all contributed a few cents each week and organized suppers in the founders' homes. And it was not politics but love that caused the death of our association. We used to go on jaunts to the outskirts of the town. It was only then that I really came to know the charm of nature in the tropics. I ate my fill of ripe and green mangos under the enormous, sweet-smelling trees; I stole sweet fresh soursops, white and red guavas, and mammee apples. And the taste of the fruit suggested to our adolescent imaginations what we thought must be the lushness and sensuality of woman. I had fallen in love with a young miss whom we called the Queen of the Plazuela del Aguila, because she lived there and there reigned in our vague desires. One day on an outing one of the club members tried to knock a slice out of a gourd that I had just cut, and on which I was carefully carving the name of my loved one. I considered his boldness an affront to my honor as a knight and to the name of my lady: after all we were living in a piratical and feudal country. There were immediate recriminations on my part and further provocations from him who, making a joke of my passion, insisted on destroying my work of art. We challenged, beat, and wounded one another. We were poisoned with an exaggerated sense of masculinity. However, I never attained the brutality of some of my companions, who amused themselves by shooting at each other with twenty-two caliber rifles. In a skirmish of this kind one of them received a grazing wound in the neck that missed his jugular vein by inches. And all this for sport, a sport that reached the proportions of real battles behind the banana groves! In our case things didn't go to such an extreme, but my father put his foot down against such barbarous activity, and the social and literary society, of which I was the most honorable treasurer, died.

In sexual matters the tropics did not push me to the extremes they did the other boys, because my weak physical nature worked as a counterbalance. On one occasion they took me in an automobile, my first ride in such a mechanical contraption —a Ford so broken down it couldn't get up Esquipulas Hill. They drove to the Cruz Verde neighborhood and stopped the car in front of a suspicious-looking house. I refused to enter. At another time my closest friend made me pass through Puerto Escondido—the street that had upset me so much before, and he ran through the street shouting to the pitiful women looking out of the doors and windows, "So much leather and I haven't enough for shoes."

In Tabasco they call prostitutes "leather," I suppose because all one is concerned with is the skin, the surface. Physically I was very far from the premature puberty of my friends; but mentally, because of our conversations, I felt pressures. One day at home when my family was away I chased my servant Isolina, a fourteen-year-old Indian girl. There would really have been a problem had I caught her because, to tell the truth, I had no idea why I was chasing her.

10

Tabascan Violence

Had the Revolution triumphed or not? I had no idea. I only knew that there was frequent gunfire. Was it between reactionaries and revolutionists? We were living in a state of great confusion, and it was difficult for a child to distinguish between the pretenders and the sincere. I observed clearly and repeatedly only two things: many high-class people were aligned with don Luis Felipe Domínguez, the conservative candidate, but they called themselves revolutionaries; the populace, especially, sided with don Carlos Greene, the revolutionary candidate, but among the leaders of this faction I noted a number of bosses and cruel overseers. I was a premature version of my father in his skeptical repudiation of political parties.

One of the shooting frays caught me on the river bank, where I was flying a "dove," a marvelous kite that the Tabascan children make with bamboo sticks and layers of rice paper. This was the pastime that I, as a self-engrossed boy, liked the most. It combined the rewards of solitude and the thrills of war. To the rag tail of the kite we tied a sharp razor, set at an angle, like a claw. We got the kites up easily, thanks to the strong wind from the Grijalva River, and once in the air there began the combat of bird against bird. At times one of them would be completely destroyed. Others dived and had to be brought down quickly, so as not to lose them in the river current or in a swamp. They were patched up with overlays of paper, and every scar was a badge of glory. Needless to say our preferred colors were those of the Mexican flag, or blue and red alone, in symbolical political combat. We also used the colors of France and Germany, then at war.

When the first shots sounded, some of the children ran, forgetting their "doves," which fell Heaven knows where; or else they tied the string to a shrub or stone, with the hope of another day running down the cord and recovering them. I couldn't abandon my glorious plaything. I retrieved it as fast as I could, winding the string haphazardly on the spool. When I had finished I was alone and I entered the city by way of Lerdo Street. On Juárez Street I came upon a group of men, pistols in hand, who recognized me. (Among them there was a friend of my family's.) They took me to my aunt's house. It was not possible for me to continue to my own home, because they wouldn't permit it. We waited a long time, hugging the wall, until my relatives opened the door for us. They took some time doing so, because they had placed the piano and various other pieces of furniture behind it to form a sort of barricade. At this moment I heard the actual whistle of the bullets for the first time.

The night I spent in my aunt's house—it was almost dark when I arrived there—was terrifying. My uncle Carlos Foucher and my cousin Juan hid a large number of bundles in the attic, packages that doubtless contained documents, bills, or deeds to property. The older persons spoke of the danger of the house being stormed. The sound of the skirmish drew nearer momentarily and occasionally, near the doors and windows, one could hear voices, orders, shouts, detonations. Only my cousin and my uncle Carlos ventured as far as the outside rooms, and especially my cousin, who had no fear of bullets, of anything or anybody. We children and the women were in the inside rooms, seated or lying on the red brick floor. I—oh, the shame of it!—was under a bed. And, on the recommendation of my aunt, I was making an effort to recite the once badly learned, and now forgotten, Lord's Prayer.

In our Tabascan families the man, even the boy, is obliged to be intrepid. It seemed to me that my cousin was regarding me with a quizzical and angry look, disgusted at my lack of fortitude. I—and I still excuse myself—was only eleven years old and, far from my father, my mother, and my sisters, was experiencing real anguish. I repeat that I don't believe my cousin was very pleased with me on this occasion. I was very weak physically, I couldn't swim across the Grijalva, I had never ridden unbroken colts and almost never went on country adventures. I was a tranquil, timid child, although not inclined to let myself be pushed around by the stronger ones; but I didn't have my cousin's fondness for the hazardous undertaking. This was doubtless a consequence of my being a male in a family of women, of being the last-born and so the pampered one, and of my lamentable rickets. I was to become brave later, because the weight of tradition was a strong one. I became brave when the smallness of my fists was no longer important, when adolescence equalized the strong and the weak. Some young men in my time carried a pistol stuck in their trousers under their blouse. I didn't do so at that time, not because I didn't wish to, but because my trip to Mexico City put off my knightly dubbing in such a fraternity. Even so, I wasn't far behind them, in spite of my civilizing transplantation: at the age of sixteen, struggling against provincial bossism, which had its representatives in the capital, I appropriated the pistol my father had left, kept it hidden, and felt myself fully capable and authorized to repel any future abuses of my physical weakness that my fierce and husky fellow-countrymen might perpetrate.

Speaking of provocations and blows sustained in this mercilessly harsh childhood, a Tabascan once remarked to me that this is a region with Greek names and a barbarous soul. What he said of the names is amusing; what he said of the soul is perhaps exaggerated and certainly tragic. To speak of the first is happiness; of the second, a lamentation.

In my region, where almost everyone was a radical, if not a positivist, people gave their children very strange names. Some of them plundered philosophy: in Tabasco there were many Socrateses, Platos, and Aristotles. Other fathers resorted to literature. On one occasion of one serenade—song and guitars at midnight at the foot of a window behind which the pale damsel supposedly awaits—there were joined the names of three Greek tragedians: Sophocles Pérez, Aeschylus Ramírez, and Euripides Guardiola. My first sweetheart was named Aziyadé, after a character of the French novelist Pierre Loti. Juliets, Desdemonas, Haydés, Nymphs, Brünnhildes, Nereids, Electras, and Sylphids gathered at the band concerts in Juárez Park. And among those I even had a friend named Belgium. Her sisters answered to the names of America, Africa, and Colombia. History provided other real finds: a relative of mine was named Emir; a girl friend, Babylonia; and others were named Ocean, Robespierre, Lincoln, Danton, and even Kuroki, after the Japanese general. History and geography books, newspapers and dictionaries were consulted by the Tabascans on the birth of a child. There were patriots who named their sons only after Juárez, the illustrious Indian patriot, or after Hidalgo, the Washington of Mexican independence, and some

Spanish Americanists called their sons Bolívar or San Martín, thinking of the great liberators of South America. A very beautiful woman, a neighbor of ours, was called Yara, after the Cuban cry of liberty of 1868. Others, less presumptuous, simply numbered their sons: Gutiérrez I, II, III, etc. Other zany individuals started with the letter "A" as the initial letter of their children's names and, if they proved prolific and exhausted the alphabet, gave them whatever outlandish name occurred to them. Also they reached the curious extreme of giving girls' names to boys and vice versa. But the Tabascan imagination, like the forests, was limitless. The wine of A. Delor and Company was sold in my father's town. The parents of one of my friends noted the name and concluded that, with some slight adjustment, it could be used as a masculine form of Adela, and so they stuck my friend with the name Adelor. Another Tabascan, a political opportunist, gave his son the name of a minister in the dictatorship: Casasús López; another that of the illustrious Cuban who organized higher education in Tabasco: Suzarte Martínez. And the Revolution was going to effect a change in fashion. In a reaction against the Christian calendar, children were called Lucifer or Mephistopheles. But in spite of all the variations and whimsies, the classical names are still the preferred: Pindar, Alcibiades, Epaminondas, Pericles, Eratosthenes, and Archimedes.

However, this remembrance of culture—not without its positive aspects to be sure, since through my childhood friend Lincoln I later became interested in the great North American president—did not prevent Harmodius and Aristogiton from drawing their pistols from their blouses and, in single combat, dying contented and smiling on the banks of the Grijalva, for love of Aspasia or Medea, or from jealousy of Andromeda or Lysistrata. And this Tabascan way of life was an indelible mark. Even in the cultured Tabascans, as in those who were only the sons or grandsons of Tabascans, it throbbed like a tempestuous and vital inner force. Even those who publicly disclaimed violence took a secret pride in the exaggerated masculinity of their people and were capable, when they listened to the voice of the forest, or riddling one another with bullets over the slightest offense. A distinguished Tabascan, a minister in don Porfirio's government, so settled a dispute at the age of sixteen. And my grandfather, one of the gentlest and most Christian Tabascans in all our history, and a sentimental poet, said softly—as I have related before—"Anyone who insults me I'll hit; anyone who hits me I'll kill." And he carried the saying to the extreme, to the point of killing, as he was dying, one of those who killed him.

The Tabascan fought and killed without realizing he was doing anything wrong. He was marked by a marvelous ingenuousness, evident in a happening I heard recounted by a brilliant and amusing friend of mine, a master of Tabascan wit and folklore. One day he visited the Villahermosa jail and there found Melchor, the foreman on his farm.

"What are you doing here, Melchor," he asked him.

"Nothing, *niño*," he replied, in his rough dialect.

"Are you a prisoner?," he inquired further, noting Melchor's disgruntled expression.

"Right, *niño*, and 'cause of a mere trifle."

And Melchor related what he considered a mere trifle.

"Just 'magine, *niño*, how that son-a-bitch of a judge Ulpiano say as how he gonna slap me wit' twenty year. You member m'sidekick Bernabé. Well he pick up he pay wit' me un right off begin t'hit the bottle. You know what a damn liquorhead he be. Drink, drink, drink, an' mo' drink. Til he start t'insult me, but *niño* I means insult me.

"But what sort of insult, what insult?," my friend asked, by now thoroughly alarmed.

"Git this. Would you b'lieve it? He say as how he handle the machete better 'an me! Scuz me if I laugh, *niño*. Just dig that sickly, pooped-out Bernabé usin' the machete better 'an me! An' me, *niño*, all the time thinkin' on me family an' takin' things real easy like, you know, coolin' it. But why drag it out? Well we leaves the sto' an' right off he ups an' say it agin, an' then we 'neath a peacock tree an' he go an' insult me agin, an' me all the while thinkin' on m'family. Then he pull out he machete an' me I pulls out me teeny, itty-bitty machete. You member how was m'lil machete, so very tiny it din't even have no edge. An' m'sidekick Bernabé he laugh, laugh, laugh. You know, he like a bro'er t'me. I godfather to he dead son Felipe. An' me laughin' too.

"But c'm on *niño*, don' git nervous. Playin', just playin', just foolin', he hit me a tiny, lil blow. An' me, just playin', me I push it off wit just the lil tip of me tiny machete. This-a-way, just like this: swish! A mere trifle, just a trifle. But who know how th̦e hell he head it fasten on, 'cause he drop off. An' don't it grab you, *niño*, to think 'cause for a lil ole nothin' like uh that, that bastard of a judge Ulpiano say he gonna gimme twenty years."

"And the bad thing about it," my friend commented, "is that not only do they kill, but they think killing is lawful and even natural."

And pity the Tabascan who didn't want to live like that! In that country there was room only for the dauntless man. The prudent man was a candidate for eternal scorn, even for death. Because in Tabasco the coward didn't live, he couldn't survive. The one who refused to fight had to be killed like a rat, like a hare, in the same spirit in which the Peloponnesians did away with deformed and sickly children, casting them from the heights of the mountain range of Taïgetos. It was not a question of just settling back and taking things easy. "If you refuse to die like a man then I'll kill you like a rabbit" was an expression heard frequently on the lips of both cultured and uncultured Tabascans. A Tabascan's adversary had to accept tragedy as a mandate of fate. If he refused, if he threw in the sponge and lived, he didn't really live, he vegetated. He was a singer in the Sistine Chapel, the eunuch of the seraglio. The sweetheart, the husband, the brother had to be worthy, with a sense of honor, and valiant to the point of heroism. Otherwise, how could sweetheart, wife, or sister possibly love him? And as a leader, only he prospered who passed unperturbedly through hails of bullets.

To be sure those rough times passed, to a degree, but honor and the worship of exaggerated masculinity remain. It can indeed be said of Tabasco, as of other regions of Mexico, that it is much like Sparta.

My Uncle Carlos

It was during that terrible night of gunfire that I first observed my uncle Carlos and Carlota carefully. I had always called her Carlota because that was the way they taught me. Since she was not married to my uncle, was neither rich nor white, I never learned to call her aunt Carlota, although she was the common-law wife, companion, and friend of my mother's brother.

My uncle was a tall man, white-skinned and strong, with a beautiful black mustache, large eyes, and a sharp nose. He always wore long, white Philippine jackets that were very becoming to him. He was the handsomest of the family. From my grandfather he inherited a name glorified by an heroic and tragic death; he likewise inherited poverty. For lack of funds he was unable to study, but of course he could have married well. He was from one of the "first families" and was a brother-in-law of the attorney Juan Martínez, who had almost as much power as the governor; he was also a brother-in-law of my father, a lawyer and judge, and of my uncle Rogerio Carpio, a doctor with excellent connections. But, a sensitive man, he scorned his aristocratic environment. How would it have been possible for him to channel his sensibility effectively in that social setting, lacking money, education, and strength of character; being, as he was by nature, somewhat of a bohemian? He was neither an intellectual, an entrepreneur, nor a man of political ambitions. Thus, instead of becoming a provincial poet and writing bad verses, he devoted himself to taking life as it came, earning just enough to live, and amusing himself openly with gambling and with certain gay ladies—this while the respectable people of Tabasco carried on clandestine love affairs with their servant girls, with girls who worked on their farms, or with the most beautiful women of the "district." But he never really went to extremes and knew how to enjoy a moderate liberty. He was a modest bureaucrat who attended provincial dances and took part in not-too-wild carousals somewhat more frequently than his companions. He was a handsome type, he belonged to a family of high social standing and—an important point—he played the flute and the guitar: these were among the reasons for his success with the ladies. Another of his diversions was to evoke the spirits: he would take a pencil, sit down in a trance and write and write. He even wrote in French, a language he didn't know, but which he had heard spoken as a child. But even this he did with an air of joking and laughter. He declared himself at a loss to explain the phenomenon scientifically, because he was very ignorant, but he didn't believe that the one moving his hand was don Porfirio. (As I mentioned before, don Porfirio was the most frequently invoked spirit.) It seemed incongruous to my uncle that that all-powerful man, who would scarcely have granted an audience to a watchman on Frontera Wharf—that is what my uncle was—would have been disposed, after death, to engage in chitchat with him.

My uncle lived in a carefree manner, without airs, and his friends were the workers of Villahermosa, who had a brotherly regard for him. I still recall the stevedore Ricardo, who treated him with great familiarity. In spite of his ties with the common people, my uncle could not join the Revolution; bloodshed horrified him. In his private life, to be sure, he lived like a revolutionist: he did what to him seemed the right thing to do; he lived frugally, quietly, and open-handedly, although he forced his family to countenance a situation that they considered reprehensible. Completely disillusioned about mankind, my uncle believed that the only two faultless attitudes were those of the ascetic or of the bohemian.

The history of my uncle's love affair is very interesting. While he was a watchman on Frontera Wharf he fell ill, and the hotel chambermaid cared for him. At that time she was a chubby, brunette girl, strong like him, with a mixture of Indian and perhaps African blood, and with the brilliant eyes of the mulatto woman. Her name was Carlota Felipe. The name perhaps derives from her Negro forebears who escaped from the Antilles and fled toward the free and tropical lands of Mexico, or from those who, once freed, followed the pirates in flight. Carlota and my uncle began living together. The Revolution, with its dangers and its hunger, united our family even more closely: this was no time for frivolous distinctions. Moreover, my family, although feudal and almost conceited, felt itself at times embued with the hospitable spirit of my grandparents. From that time on Carlota Felipe and my uncle Carlos lived with my Martínez cousins. This meant that my family, identified with the conservative counterrevolution, was tolerating in their home—oh, the horror of it!—what everyone called a concubinage.

My uncle Carlos, the son of a governor, of French blood and related to the best families of Tabasco, in his union with Carlota Felipe, a mulatto charwoman, made a happier match than did any of the other children of the legendary provincial poet. When they were apart, they wrote to each other every day. He had taught her to write so as not to be without her letters, and they exchanged the most tender sentiments. Such a marriage could only have been fashioned from the freedom, spontaneity, and naturalness of my uncle—qualities that proved stronger than those prevailing in his period and his surroundings.

12

The Revolution Betrayed?

My sister's illness kept pushing us toward the highest part of the town in search of purer air, fleeing the humidity and miasmas of the river. We lived at first on Juárez Street, on the top floor of a three-story house. Later we moved to the very highest point in the town, to a two-story house on Encarnación Hill. That flight from the swamp—from malaria and tuberculosis—was to end quickly and tragically in Mexico City.

I had no friends in that section and, with the imminence of the trip to the capital, I stopped attending school. There—as always happened when I was alone—I was content. From the high flat roof, thanks to a marvelous wind, I could fly my kites. I could climb onto the roof of the Masonic Temple, which was at the height of our patio, and spy through the skylights to observe the ceremonies and aprons of which I had been told and which excited me greatly; and, in search of engravings and books, I could poke around my father's library, which was gradually being restored.

There I read *The Intervention and the Empire*, by Salado Alvarez. The four volumes, bound in red Spanish leather with gilt edges, absorbed my attention and helped to define my already radical patriotism. Pancho and Miguel Caballero de los Olivos, heroes of the war against the French Intervention, captivated me and increased the chill I always felt upon listening to the Mexican national anthem. Miguel's mother-in-law and her daughter, wasp-waisted women with amply endowed busts, enthralled my imagination and relegated to the second echelon the muslin-clad young women I saw in Tabasco. The book made me eager for the trip to the plateau of Mexico City; it captivated me with the photographs of its palaces, its promenades, its churches. And it was a further boost for my childish worship of Porfirio Díaz, because it depicted the heroic Porfirio, faithful friend, who wept before the cold body of Pancho Caballero de los Olivos—whom I so admired—and accorded him the funeral honors of a general. There I also read a few of the *National Episodes* of the Spanish novelist Galdós, and became acquainted with the French writer Zola: a translation of *The Downfall* didn't make me hate war, but inclined me toward dreaming of my own sacrifice on the altars of my native country. And I started to read another of his works, *Rome*, but I couldn't get through more than five pages of its descriptions. Also I read *The Sun of May* and *The Hill of Bells* by the Mexican author Juan A. Mateos, as well as *The Magic Lantern* of Facundo, all of which increased my curiosity about the metropolis. One day I glanced at *Mexico Across the Centuries*. And in a cabinet I found an engraving, "Leda and the Swan," which nourished my precocious concupiscence.

At this time my father began to take me more seriously, and

I started to assist him in his office as a typist. I still recall our mutual displeasure because in a document he dictated to me I several times wrote "imperiment" for "impediment." I always got a bad taste in my mouth when I saw him get angry. A client who witnessed the scene took on my simple defense and smoothed things over. I also assumed the grave responsibility of knowing the combination of the safe in which he kept money and documents belonging to his clients: I considered myself its zealous guardian. With such a gracious upgrading of my personality and responsibilities, I felt myself authorized to give my opinion on all topics. On seeing a rather indifferent picture in my father's office in which the Germans were symbolized by a strong bull surrounded by twenty trembling and cowardly bullfighters, I proclaimed myself a Germanophile. That business of "twenty against one," that I had heard so often in the school when some student was being bullied by the others, as well as the fierce and mustachioed engraving of the Kaiser, were very important to my childish reasoning. And the popular verses of the time also molded my thinking. One in particular made me imagine that I was Germany, harassed by twenty boys from my elementary school.

My reading and my status as my father's collaborator and stampkeeper so inflated me that I reached the extreme of falling romantically in love with a little neighbor girl of ours who was always to be seen on the balcony facing our office and who answered, like a true miss of Tabasco, to the outlandish name of Venusia; I even composed an acrostic in her honor.

I lived through some bloody events there too. One day elections were held to decide between Domínguez and Greene, and from this I learned a marvelous lesson about the democratic process. At ten in the morning my cousin Pánfilo, the owner of the millinery shop, appeared with a pistol in his belt, a heavy club in his hand, and a wild glint in his eyes. He was a conservative. A little later I saw one of my Pombo uncles pass by in a similar getup, on his way to the polling booths. The election had a farcical beginning: from the river banks the two parties brought legions of peasants, whom they proceeded to get drunk in the streets. Then there followed an altercation about who was, and who was not, registered. The polling booths were contested with club blows, and at noon the shots began. Some stray bullets hit the high walls of my house, and the result of all this was a week of general anxiety. I don't know whether it was then or later that they killed the father of the interim governor, whose funeral procession I saw pass by the corner of my house. I only know that everyone's mouth hung open in stark panic.

On one of those days they knocked at my door. My mother peeked out one of the windows, closed it carefully and said, "It's the reds." I took a look and saw a patrol, all the members of which wore the revolutionary insignia on their shirts. My father was suffering at that time from a severe case of jaundice; the color of his face was scarcely in harmony with the circumstances, but on the other hand it was not compromising, since it was yellow. He got up and ordered us to open the door at once. Fortunately it was Andrés Pombo, son of that rebel uncle whose life my father had saved during the time of Victoriano Huerta. He said that the disgruntled conservatives, led by Leónidas, the son of the defeated candidate, were thinking of attacking the city by shelling it from the river. He had come to take us to his house, which was safer because, among other things, it was inhabited by reds, offered less of a target, and was made of stone. My father preferred for us to stay where we were, repeating as always that he had nothing to fear.

Many strange things were related about that election struggle. It was recounted that my uncle Casiano, the conservative, had clubbed his rebel brother Pablo at the height of the melee. When he saw him on the ground he dismounted—they were both on horseback during the fight—picked him up, doubled him over his horse's neck and took him lovingly to his house, where the two of them and their families were living at the time. There, wives, sisters-in-law, and nieces treated his bump with hydrogen peroxide, arnica, and iodine. Truth or falsehood, we fed on those glorious and edifying stories.

A little later it was declared officially that the revolutionary candidate, Carlos Greene, had won and he accordingly received the governorship from the one who had held it provisionally. Was the Revolution succeeding? Certain measures were being taken that attempted to indicate that it was. One of these involved my father.

One day an official notice came from the government in which he was ordered to turn over his library to the Instituto Juárez so that the poor students could make use of it in their studies. His library at the time consisted of two or three hundred volumes, remnants of what had been lost in 1914. The greater and best part of that collection had remained in the hands of the opportunists of those tumultuous times, those who had taken advantage of the prevailing popular fury to gather up the books lying in the street as "spoils of war," or who had bought them at the ridiculous prices the peasants put on them: five *centavos* for a book with pictures; one *centavo* for a book without pictures. My father had been able to recover only a few volumes, almost none complete, and none of value as a school text. He went to the government officials and explained the situation to them. Even so they demanded the library—the phantom library—and to comply would have meant to replace it from the bookstores of Mexico City. He couldn't, and didn't, do this, because he had no money, and because he left Tabasco shortly afterwards.

My attention was attracted by other contradictions and injustices in the Revolution. Was it triumphant or wasn't it? I became aware of the wealth of certain individuals who called themselves revolutionaries, and I began to witness the mockery of promises solemnly made in the meetings. The people themselves were losing confidence in the leaders and were beginning to show their bitterness.

"They're not revolutionaries but robberlutionaries," I heard a fruit vendor remark.

They called robbing "Carranzaizing." The name of don Venustiano, an honest man, had become the victim of the corruption of some of his adherents. My old nurse Paula, rowdy and foul-mouthed, insulted, in my presence, a group of officers as they passed by the house: "At least we had something to eat before. Now all you think about is your 'advances.' Ay, son of a bitch!"

To "advance" did not have a military connotation here; it was simply another of the countless verbs meaning to "steal." A bad sign indeed when the word had so many synonyms. Moreover, I saw a drayman on Juárez Street being driven to jail with whip and club for having suggested that there were thieving leaders.

"Just like during the damned dictatorship," I heard a group of reds commenting.

There were many other measures designed to mask the truth, like the attempt to appropriate my father's library—an effort to make people believe that the government was genuinely concerned about the poor students' having good books at their disposal. There were other acts that also demonstrated the weakening of the Revolution and its premature disappearance.

I recall some painful cases. During the Greene administration someone decreed that everything that had been seized in 1914 was to be returned. As a result, some of what had been lost at that time came back to the house. Cholita, a poor working girl who lived near us and who, when the house was ransacked, took a china doll that had belonged to my sisters, came one day to return it. For this poor girl the Revolution had been a shining dream and a cruel awakening. Things were getting back to their former status quo. But the drama of Lucho Pérez was the most moving of all. He was a poor boy, a saddler's son as I recall, with a great fondness for the piano, but with no place to study. With the triumph of the Revolution our piano was taken and ended up in his house. Upon our return he did everything possible to hide it, but to no avail, because everyone knew where it was.

"It's at Lucho's house," those who had remained hidden in Villahermosa during the popular uprising whispered to us. They had even communicated this fact by letter while we were traveling about Campeche in the period of our involuntary tourism: "Lucho Pérez stole the piano." The hour for rectifications arrived and the piano returned to my house. But I was greatly astonished to learn that Lucho, at my father's invitation, would be coming to the house to practice on it. Some of our friends were outraged. My father explained that he wasn't giving the piano to Lucho because he didn't have the money to buy another for my sisters. Lucho came, a little timid and nervous, once or twice, but that was all, although my father sat down attentively to listen to him play, then applauded and chatted with him. The trouble was we spied on him, and in our already cruel young eyes he was able to discern the insults of our selfishness. He realized that we, who didn't really care about the piano or even want it, resented his coming to use it. The rebellious people of 1914 lapsed again into submission. They returned our piano, the dolls, the furniture and, at the same time, the government was asking my father for a library that did not exist. With all this my father, Cholita, and Lucho Pérez were being humiliated. As a result of such a welter of contradictions, I began to shake off my perplexities and evolve a counterrevolutionary attitude, anti-Greene in substance, because I had heard it said in the meetings that Greene *was* the Revolution. This was a very grave error that as yet I was unable to correct, and one in which many adult and lucid minds were ensnared. I asked myself why this man, the leader of the reds, of the Revolution, and ostensibly the friend of the people, acted in such a contradictory manner. Weren't the two official orders—those involving the restitution of the seized property and the commandeering of my father's nonexistent

library—false and farcical? Just where was the Revolution?
Who and what, actually, was the leader Greene? Wasn't he, in
these various maneuvers, really playing both sides of the political street? It was said that once, when someone was discussing I don't know what orders with Greene and citing the constitutional guarantees and laws of 1917, Greene responded,
"There is no other law here than that of my breeches."
I never met Greene and am not really in a position to judge
him. But that is what I saw and heard, what they made me see
and hear. And so for me that was the Revolution.
I was against sham, falsehood, and injustice. But these were
not really the Revolution; rather they represented the crisis,
or deviation, and human failures of the Revolution—something
I was unable to understand. I was fully prepared to recognize
its shortcomings but not its accomplishments. Moreover, my
father—honorable, generous, tender, hard-working, sober, and
unassuming—was being labeled a reactionary and a Porfirista.
As a result, in my childish reasoning, I equated reaction and
Porfirismo with the good and the Revolution with the bad. I
believed and declared myself to be a Porfirista and a reactionary, although I had received from my parents as fundamental
lessons the doing of good, love for the people, and defense of
the oppressed.
One day our doctor in Villahermosa, convinced that my
sister would soon die, spoke out clearly and declared her condition to be a grave one. My mother's old idea, that she should
go to Mexico City for treatment, was accepted, and she, my
sister, and I set out for the capital.

13

Mexico City

In Frontera I saw for the last time the great Grijalva River, which enters the Gulf disgorging the water from its two enormous branches, and embarked on a large launch, the "Papantla," to challenge the terrible sea.

To make the trip from Frontera to Veracruz in such boats, veritable eggshells powered by dilapidated motors and guided by seamen living in a state of potential suicide on a paltry salary, was indeed an adventure; ours was a dreadful one. A nor'easter jolted us shortly after putting to sea. Great waves swept the deck; the vessel would at one moment be submerged in the black and menacing waters, and at the next become the crest of a foaming, rough, and tumbling mountain. I made out the silhouettes of the passengers against the dark sky or in the ink-black waters. The men waited, staunchly silent, grasping the rails of the boat; the women, lashed together, prayed or cried out. The seasickness of the early hours had given way to fear, the strongest of emotions. My mother, my sisters, a dentist friend, and I were in the captain's stateroom. It seemed that almost everyone had turned Catholic; it was St. Joseph's Day and they were invoking him. It was the first time I regretted not knowing how to cross myself in the complicated manner then used in Mexico. Calm finally prevailed, and the men, as we approached Puerto México, where we were to make an emergency landing because of damage to our boat, amused themselves by firing their pistols at the frustrated sharks following the boat.

In Puerto México, of which my only recollection is the delicious white, watery *jícama* root that I bought in a stall on the wharf, we waited for another boat and continued our journey toward Veracruz.

I remember Veracruz as everyone from the provinces recalls a large city. I was coming from Villahermosa—almost a village —and my recollection of Mérida was by now vague and remote. As a result Veracruz had, perforce, to seem like a metropolis to me. Here I learned about adultery, as a result of the love affair that an uncle of mine (you can see that I have uncles in the four corners of the world), a famous lawyer in the port, was having with a foreign lady. My family was greatly attracted by the exotic! Here too I became aware of sexual inversion, because the students in the boarding house where we stayed made fun of our servant, a consummate fairy; as they did also—because of his large, dyed mustache—of the Mexican poet Díaz Mirón, whom I came upon one day seated on a park bench, crouching in a sulk, holding a kerchief in the hand twisted by a bullet he had received in one of his bloody quarrels. Those persons, and a horse-drawn coach that almost ran me down, form my principal recollections of the port.

On the other hand the trip to the capital impressed me very

little, in spite of the beautiful things to be seen on the way. I was in the midst of a much more moving and absorbing spectacle: that of my grieving mother and my gravely ill sister, racked by tuberculosis, on her way to Mexico City in search of an impossible cure. The move to the capital was also important for me, because it meant a change from the picturesque and radiant life of the tropics to the pale and regimented life of a great city.

Feeling, thinking, and suffering were going to cloud the spectacle of the capital, just as the Revolution had before clouded my view of nature. The struggle between men—violent death, bloodshed, and unleashed passions—had been a blindfold that kept me from appreciating, even noticing, the beauty of our great rivers, of our marvelous beaches, or the green countryside of Tabasco. My parents' grief, our poverty during the Revolution, and later our common anguish over my sister's death helped make me even more of a self-engrossed, introverted child.

Doctor Hugo Topf's elementary school, that I entered as a boarding student, could not distract me from the lingering drama of my sister's six-month agony. I witnessed the failures of all the great doctors of Mexico City and the collapse of my parents' hopes, which, in desperation, they finally placed in quacks.

My sister Julieta was a sweet, timid, melancholy girl, with skin as white as wax, as transparent as paraffin. She was the most beautiful of all the women in our family and the most European in type, with her pale skin and delicate features. She seemed almost predestined for an early death by her downheartedness toward life, her scorn for material things, her love of seclusion, and her pronounced and silent sensitiveness. Marked by a spiritual, immaterial, almost intangible beauty, she was one of those few cases in which physical purity is not a lack of reverence toward the natural demands of the flesh, nor a disregard of the rights of youth. And all of this was spontaneous, without any trace of mysticism or confessional virtue. My cousin Romeo—perhaps *because* he was named Romeo—loved her and had the romantic luck to have her fall ill with a disease of the chest. I watched that life slip away. Every two weeks I went home and she, very gently, almost without breathing and scarcely touching me, fearing to infect me, would kiss me on the forehead. She accepted the idea of pain and death with the fortitude characteristic of my father's secularism. Only once, like the flutter of a candle about to be extinguished, she gave way to despair and said that she didn't want to die; but she always accepted her misfortune without supernatural fears or hopes. While she lay dying, some young girls, friends of ours, healthy and joyful, were singing, laughing, and skating at the door of our house. Those voices of youth and life did not, however, cause her to lose her resignation. She knew no other love than the brotherly and tender affection of her cousin Juan. He passed the anguished days of her destruction, with my parents, at her bedside.

One day my cousin Romeo came to my school crying. I had endured many hours of impatience because my vacation had begun and nobody had come to get me. From the second-floor corridor, which commanded a view of the door, I set up my watch and passed the exasperating days, hoping to catch a glimpse of my father's black felt hat. I hadn't gone to my house for a month, and for three weeks had had no word from there. For some days I had noted a strange silence in my roommates. Then my cousin Romeo came up to my room, found a black necktie and put it on me. Afterwards he took me to the Hotel Colonia on Jalapa Street where my parents were waiting for me. My sister Julieta had died.

I spent the six months of my sister's terminal illness in Doctor Topf's school in the Santamaría district. It was a lay school. Don Joaquín Balcárcel, the director, a liberal, cordial but energetic man, made me shed my ways as a pampered child. I also began to lose, bit by bit, my good old Tabascan rusticity. The new environment, morally superior to the one I had left, kept filing away the spurs of my tropical childhood, but this only slowly and laboriously. Like the blast of a forge, the aura of Tabasco welds the spirit of its sons, even when they are in the capital or in a foreign country. I was scornful of the boys of the metropolis, gentler than the Tabascans, at times sanctimoniously prayerful, and who displayed their bare legs in short socks, since they did not wear the long, stretch-cotton stockings to which I was accustomed. As far as I was concerned, attendance at Mass and short socks constituted unquestionable proof of effeminacy. Carrión, a stout young fellow who wore them, replied to that opinion of mine with a challenge to a fight. I managed to extricate myself from this because María, one of the servants at the school and the one who liked me most, burst into the patio where we were meeting and drove off my adversary, much my superior physically, with a broom. Fentanes and Villafaña, who also knew how to fight with kicks like Tabascans, always held me at bay. One day when Rosas—a boy from Orizaba, five or six years older than I—tried to hit me, I stood up to him with belt blows; however, he, with his own belt buckle, inflicted such a deep wound on my left hand that it bared the bone and caused a bad hemorrhage. My cousin Luciano, who drove a small Ford taxi, was indignant upon learning that I had been frightened by the blood. He informed me that real men, like himself, rather got angry when they were wounded. As a sort of compensation for my faintheartedness I gave Múzquiz, nephew of the director and of don Venustiano Carranza, a kick in the rear just for the hell of it. After each fight the director would call us and, looking deep into our eyes, give us a bone-crushing handshake as a punishment. However, he never chastised us cruelly, never raised his voice, and never responded to the worst faults or acts of my companions with violent gesture or bitter word. His rectitude—which we admired—and his Veracruz cordiality were complemented by the tenderness of his wife, Virginia

Lobo. We looked upon her as an intelligent mother, and cherished our daily and fraternal relations with their children Celia, Ana María, Popo, Carmela, Juacho, and Virginia. In that modest school, with a student body living as a family—some fifty boys—under the direction of a true teacher, we received the best possible of educations.

The students, as was to be expected, completed my sexual education. I lived on the second floor with the older and precocious boys like myself. What with the serious and specific explanations of my Professor Alvarez, and those of my roommates, I finally harbored no more doubts. Perhaps owing to this fact, because of the change of climate, and because of my obsession with the suffering of my sister and my parents, my sexual restlessness subsided and almost disappeared for several years. When I used to go home, Mercedes, a chubby little maid, used to kiss me a great deal. I, neither reticent nor lazy, explored her body, but with the almost exclusive intention of "verifying" my recently acquired knowledge.

"What are you looking for? What are you looking for?" she used to ask me. I really didn't know, but that did not disturb my tranquility. Imagination, the better part of sensuality —particularly at an age when only that part could exist—had been fully satisfied.

14

The Colegio Mexicano

It was with great regret that I abandoned Doctor Hugo Topf's school, my masculine life among simple, provincial boys, the suppers of rice and beans that we consumed with such hearty appetites, and my cross-eyed Professor Alvarez, the best prepared teacher of all those I had in primary school. My sisters came from Tabasco and the family took up residence in the Roma district. I finished my fifth year of school and began my sixth, as a day student, in the Colegio Mexicano.

This had been established in the splendid building occupied by the former boarding school. It soon attracted hundreds of students. It was aided by the prestige and excellent connections of don Joaquín Balcárcel who, for promotional purposes, was its nominal Director, as well as by the resources of various financial partners who, unfortunately, were the real directors. It was founded with a great deal of political and financial acumen. By this time the Revolution had created its own aristocracy. Elements of it that I, a boy still a panegyrist of Porfirio Díaz, came to know there had all the vices of the old aristocracy, plus the cynicism of calling itself revolutionary. It loved the good life, the binge, and luxury as had its predecessor. The old Porfirista aristocracy did not as yet entirely accept the new. It half rejected it in spite of the fact that, in reality, it had had an exactly similar origin: that is to say, each had, in its time, struggled against social injustice. As a matter of fact there were only differences of age between the two, but they viewed one another with hostility. The members of the new aristocracy, born of the Revolution, either did not wish to or could not, for one reason or another, send their boys to the elite schools that the children of the others attended: the English, the Franco-English, the French, or German schools—nor to the public schools either. Then the Colegio Mexicano was established, no less expensive than, and at least equally as pretentious as, the others. All of the new aristocracy attended this school: sons of generals, of nouveaux riches, of distinguished plunderers of the national budget. Of course there were also boys with names of honorable revolutionary leaders. Then, too, all those fathers chose it who did not wish to send their sons to either the religious or foreign schools, and among these was my own father. These reasons—plus the general distrust and prejudice regarding official education—caused many social sectors to be ensnared by the advertising of the Colegio Mexicano.

Managed by extremely clever businessmen, it made some astonishingly successful opportunistic moves: it increased the role of sports, remembered the Indian, directed North American influence to its ends, and espoused a radical social justice in the direction of a false and spectacular racism.

There were basketball, football, and baseball teams; there

was an enormous swimming pool where weekly contests were
held in diving and long-distance and speed swimming; there
was fencing and boxing—just as in a large North American
university. Except for the fact that the emphasis on sports was
exaggerated, one would have to say that in this area it was a
great school, for it produced some of the best Mexican ath-
letes. But in the final analysis it was little more than a muscle
factory. There I completed the sixth year of elementary instruction and the first of the preparatory course—but got little
or nothing out of it. Oh, for my modest but capable provincial
teachers; oh, for my Doctor Hugo Topf's elementary school,
with its modest building and our beloved cross-eyed Professor
Alvarez, who taught us so well and instilled such high ideals
in our minds with *Hearts*, de Amicis' unforgettable book.
Naturally, the students' fathers, in a majority of cases pretentious parvenus, cared less than nothing whether their sons
studied or not. The essential thing was that they be in a good
school, an expensive and beautiful one, with "aristocratic"
people, and that they pass the courses. This last point presented no problems: that was what they were paying for. As
long as the influence of don Joaquín lasted—which was not a
great while because he resigned and never returned—there
were some good teachers. But because of a boxing match between Fernando Capdevielle and Luis Herrera Montes, or
because of a basketball game, classes were suspended and
Schulz, Ayala, Baz, and all the good teachers took off. There
was the rub. Moreover, physical education was imparted
without prior physical examination, to the fat, the thin, the
strong, and the weak. As a result I was forced to defend myself—inventing illnesses and missing classes—from that lethal
daily fatigue and from the embarrassing and continual exhibi-
tion of my pitiful skeleton. That passion for "vigor," that was
nothing short of a farce and a servile aping of North American ways, caused the school to engage cheap, terribly incom-
petent teachers who simply vegetated, safely intrenched under

the reputations of four or five excellent ones. It was also responsible for one of my professor's performing certain chemical experiments that became famous: like pouring various acids helter-skelter into a test tube and producing an intolerable stench up to a half-mile away, or frightening us with unexpected explosions, or saying, as he stuck his razor into the strange mixture, "Let's see what happens to the razor." One day it turned into something resembling twisted candy.

The farce centered about the Indian was at once the cruelest and the most ludicrous. The directors of the school—save don Joaquín, who always remained aloof and disgusted—continually declared that they "stood for the postulates of the Revolution," and they were among those who would have it appear that "it is necessary to consider the Indian right even though he isn't." They never taught us in Mexico that the defense of the Indian, by virtue of his being the base of the social pyramid, should be identified with the defense of the exploited man as such. We were told, rather, that he had to be elevated as an Indian and not as an exploited individual. As a result, people wished to elaborate in his name, as has so often been done, a vacuous and exaggeratedly patriotic concept: the struggle against the *criollo*. Except that the attacks that the demagogues, false friends of the Indian, opportunistically directed against everyone who was not an Indian, fell flat when they observed the white skin of the sons of some of the northern revolutionary chieftains, for example those of President Venustiano Carranza and of General Alvaro Obregón. The Revolution, which at no time was racist in nature, which was against neither the Indian nor the white Mexican, was fought in the press and on the field of battle by Indians, *mestizos*, and whites, as simple soldiers or as military and civilian leaders.

But the marvelous thing was when the directors, diligent in their desire to pass as revolutionaries and friends of the people, brought two Indian boys from Oaxaca to study in their school and "make men of them." They were two young, observant, and determined Zapotecans. They were soon numbered among the best students and we liked them very much. But we couldn't help feeling a certain compassion for them because there was no function they were allowed to miss, were it a dance, an awarding of prizes, or the opening of classes. They always seated them, dressed in gaudy fashion, on the proscenium, where they had to endure the fulsome phrases of the official speakers: "You, the mother race, will be rehabilitated." "By protecting you we trample on three hundred years of theocracy, obscurantism, and barbarism." And ad nauseam. Invariably the orator spoke of the goodness of the school's directors, to whom he referred as "true revolutionaries, protectors of the Indian, like the gentle missionary Bartolomé de las Casas." From that moment I recognized the political trick, the advantageous lie. Because the two Zapotecans again became servants as soon as the invited guests had departed, and worked out their expenses cleaning even the toilets. The two boys were the director's best servants: they were paid nothing and served as a political snare. And long live the Revolution!

The cynicism of Mexican youth, like that of their parents, was greater in Mexico City than in Tabasco. I noticed this in the Colegio Mexicano. In Doctor Hugo Topf's school I was not aware of it: there my boarding-school companions were the sons of provincials, generally professionals or ranchers of Veracruz or Oaxaca, and the day students, save in exceptional cases, were of modest circumstances. In the Colegio Mexicano my companions led the life of their families, which were generally rich or at least well-to-do, and they reflected that atmosphere. In the capital, as the center of the country, as the province of the victors, of the most clever, the desire for possessions and the desire to show off reached their highest point. The children were a reflection of the city and repeated what they heard and saw.

I did not have an automobile. This fact was the touchstone. The boys knew my father was a magistrate. One day Drivel—

a boy we had so nicknamed because he drooled—called to me.

"What's eating you, Drivel," I asked him.

"How come you don't have a car, Hothead, and your father a judge?"

"Because my father is honest."

"Don't give me that! If your father doesn't steal, he's a sucker."

Drivel, like me, was thirteen innocent years old.

My natural reaction to such slurs and jokes was to boast of my father's integrity, and the modesty of my clothes compared to the elegance of my classmates.

Someone was talking one day about the money it would take to buy two pairs of boxing gloves, basketball equipment, a copy of *The Treasury of Youth*, and other childish whims, and was complaining about not having everything he wanted, as, for example, did the son of the attorney Coyote or of Colonel Forrajes. There was much concern about money and the need to come by it.

"Just put me where it's at," said cropped-headed Chávez.

"Have power, in order to have," declared Palomera, one of the older boys in the class.

Such phrases were common coin in the mouths of the youth, as were also the classic questions:

"How much does your father earn?"

"And the graft?"

"And the shady deals?"

The boys were already using a lexicon of piracy.

I followed politics attentively as always, but scarcely read the newspapers. I remember that by chance I learned of the death of Emiliano Zapata and of General Felipe Angeles. I greeted these notices without emotion: the Revolution had enraptured me in another period, in Tabasco, listening to the rebel leaders; but I became disenchanted with it as a result of the cruel treatment I received at the hands of my revolutionary teacher Chin Chun Chan. What I did notice though, on my way to school, were the houses of the generals and the lawyers, the fathers of my friends, almost all of the houses luxurious, with great gardens always filled with men carrying pistols. A general lived on my own street, and at night several friends and I tried to observe through the windows the carousals that he and his friends celebrated in the company of elegant-looking women. For our part we lived in a five-room apartment in the humblest and most uninhabited section of the Roma district. I pointed out to my friends that they, as the sons of revolutionists, lived in comfortable houses while I, the son of a conservative, lived in a modest apartment. I asked them how this could be and they answered cynically,

"What do you think we were fighting for, Hothead?"

One day I noticed strange preparations at the house of my neighbor, the general. I also observed similar activity at the house of another general—very young and foppish—on Chihuahua Street. There were many soldiers about, busy carrying out bundles, and a large number of automobiles arrived. An old lady was crying in my neighbor's house. What was going on? I got the answer a few days later: Carranza had been assassinated in Tlaxcalantongo, and another group was coming from Sonora to take command.

Classes were suspended at the school. With Quijano and Ruiseco, my best friends, I went to Chapultepec Park to hunt birds with slingshot. The park was deserted, there were no policemen, no gamekeepers, and very few visitors. For the boys and the couples who disappeared into the grove that was heaven. Later I passed by the school and the servants told me of the most recent happenings: they had shot Tom's and Dick's fathers; on the other hand, Harry's father was more important than ever and was going to be a minister; and so-and-so's father was the one who had shot it out with Dr. Camarena. Although tragic, none of this news was particularly edifying, and it was of a sort that I could now hear with absolute impassivity as I sucked on my lemon ice cream cone. Some of the boys' fathers died and they left the school. Others, whose fathers made it big and now had larger, newer cars, returned to the school much happier. In the meantime my father continued in judicial posts, and we went on living with the customary frugality. One day we left the apartment and took a small, two-story house, also quite modest, but which seemed like a palace to us. It had a very high flat roof where I could smoke with my cousins and from where, with our twenty-two rifles, we shot holes in the water storage tanks of our neighbors and got into other kinds of mischief.

My sisters were no longer studying the piano, but were attending a business school and taking typewriting and bookkeeping. My father knew that some day they would have to earn their living. He was not about to secure the family's future by selling a decision in his civil court. Sometimes strange people came to my house, soldiers and guerrilla leaders, who tried to induce my father to stand for election to the governorship of my province. Another my fifty thousand uncles, still the rebel and conspirator of always, and who shortly after took part in an uprising and was shot or assassinated in Oaxaca, tried in vain to get him to lead an armed revolt. My father paid no attention to any of them.

"No, neither with the government nor with the opposition," he declared, shaking his noble head. "One man can't do everything, and I would be practically alone. I wouldn't want them to kill me, and much less would I wish to kill anyone, were I not sure that such terrible sacrifices would be fruitful. I can't see their usefulness. For that reason I am still what I was, a lawyer. As a judge I dispense justice and try to combat injustice. It's not much, I know, but it is something tangible, certain, and satisfactory."

The propagandists and conspirators left with their tails between their legs. My own life and that of my family continued in a world apart, mere spectators of the tragedies of the Revolution, blind and deaf before its accomplishments. We were still, without question, Porfiristas.

One event that did move me greatly was the funeral of don Venustiano Carranza, which Ruiseco and I attended as onlookers. We accompanied the cortège briefly and went on to his home in the Cuauhtémoc district. We observed and sympathized with the old friends that were with the family. There were broken leaves and flowers on the ground, sobs, tears, drawn faces, distinguished and humble women moaning on friends' breasts. We called down the wrath of Heaven on the assassins. I had seen don Venustiano a short time before, perhaps the fifth of the previous May, in a parade I witnessed with a cousin of mine on Madero Avenue. He was riding in his car, erect, strong, elegant, and dignified, his hand stroking his beautiful beard. At my side an angry-faced man muttered, "The old son of a bitch . . ."

I left the scene of the funeral reflecting on the price one paid for power. I reflected too on the fact that there were men as good as my father in the Revolution, families like my own. But again the old contradiction: the very death of don Venustiano and the doleful picture of his family further ingrained my errors—he had been sacrificed because he was the only honorable one. For if don Venustiano, brave and upright as he was, had been assassinated, that meant to me, quite simply, that the Revolution had been betrayed. As far as I was concerned they were all still cruel rogues, and now I could add that they were traitors too, for having killed don Venustiano. I couldn't be a rebel because I was neither a rogue, cruel, nor a traitor. I was a reactionary because I wanted all men to be equal, to eat and dress equally, and I wanted our leaders to be educated, honorable, and loyal like my father. That was the essence of my reactionism. Because of my hatred of political corruption, which I had observed in my school, and my aversion to bloodshed, which had impressed me especially with the death of

Carranza, I rejected the Revolution and made it responsible for all crimes. In all this confusion, one truly reactionary concept stood out: my excessive esteem for the white race, my racism, my Aryanism, that attributed to the Indian, the basis of the national population, all defects. And perhaps in my strange attraction to don Venustiano, whom I had heard vituperated during all my childhood in Tabasco, his European beard played a part. And I still harbored an erroneous feeling: my untoward admiration for General Porfirio Díaz because he did not steal, because he had fought against the French, and because he had made Mexico admired in Europe. To correct my errors in judgment and values I needed contacts other than those I found in the Colegio Mexicano.

My father had come to realize the frivolous character of the school. He called it a fools' showcase and factory for producing hoity-toity children. I finished my sixth year, and it was then decided that I would enroll in the National Preparatory School.

But, unfortunately, we first-year students did not attend the large school, the old Colegio de San Ildefonso, whose simple magnificence would have been enough to enthrall and encourage me. We were confined in the so-called "doghouse"—for the "curs" of the first year—in the old monastery of San Pedro and San Pablo. Moreover, we were a veritable army that overflowed the classrooms; we were a motley, heterogeneous crew, of all extractions and odors. It was the odors that repelled me. Many of my companions were very poor boys, and we were still living in a period when the humble classes of Mexico City bathed very little. This was true even of the city boys who had a house with a bathroom. Because of poverty or tradition my companions knew nothing about cleanliness. Sometimes I thought I would faint in class. Being from the tropics, I had always bathed daily in my province, and in Mexico City with a frequency respectful of other noses. I viewed with panic the movement of the boy's feet behind me, for no sooner did he shift them than they emitted a latrine-

like stench. In addition there was much disorder in the classes
owing to the unexpected number of students. Don José Vasconcelos was then Minister of Education, and among the
poorer classes there was an increasing desire to study, as a result of his campaign in favor of popular culture. One day I
belonged to group "A," but the teacher sent me to "B," and
the teacher of "B" turned me out and sent me to "C" or "D."
I belonged to four groups and to none. There were conflicts
in the matter of class hours that caused me to lose time and patience. I was a quiet boy, not given to discussion, without
great initiative, and I didn't know how to arrange my sched-
ule in the office of the Secretary. It was a real crisis of bash-
fulness and timidity. Perhaps also it was a question of adolescence. I was confused, discouraged, and benumbed. My
father sensed the situation and, with great disgust and reluc-
tance, but convinced of my inability to overcome the change
of atmosphere and customs, asked me if I would like to return
to the Colegio Mexicano. I said that I would, and two weeks
later I was again in that superficial, pretentious, class-con-
scious school, but one in any event that was quiet and familiar
to me.

The confusion continued. I was at ease neither with those
who smelled bad on the outside nor with those who stank on
the inside. My congenital ineptitude in mathematics earned me
the enmity of the director of studies leading to the bachelor's
degree, and my greatest torture was attendance at his classes
in mathematics and algebra. A great diffidence had replaced
all my former precocious sexual boldness. There were girls in
the Colegio Mexicano and they, seated in the front row were,
to a degree, responsible for the mental confusion I suffered
when confronting logarithms. But I found great solace in the
French course with Salvador Grosso; in the Spanish course of
don Leopoldo Ayala; and in that in drawing of Del Valle, in
all of which I recovered my lost powers. Naturally I passed
mathematics: that's what one paid for. But, without doubt,

some sort of deception must have been practiced on the brilliant and terrible examiner, Professor López Aguado, who came from the government preparatory school to test us. Because without some sort of hanky-panky I couldn't have gotten through: I didn't even understand first degree equations. I followed my classes without interest. My attention fluttered like a butterfly between shyness in the presence of the girl students, fear of the director, and enthusiasm for film stars like William Duncan and Juanita Hansen, who at that moment were hypnotizing me with "The Broken Coin." That was the period of the great serial pictures: Eddie Polo and Antonio Moreno were other of the preferred actors. The movies distracted me from the embarrassing situation at the school and made me admire, with a dual admiration—childish and Tabascan—the heroic acts portrayed on the screen. The Yankee West of films was not very different from the country where I was born and where I passed my childhood. The heroes of the North American West were twin brothers of some of my uncles in Tabasco.

Student politics reached the Colegio Mexicano. As in Tabasco, there were revolutionaries and conservatives. I was an enemy of the revolutionary candidate because he was, or aspired to be, the sweetheart of a cousin of mine. That was enough for me to hate him according to my still medieval ethics. And I was a conservative because my cousin Juan was one of the leaders of this group. The orator who spoke for those sporting the red ribbon was a verbose and pedantic student from my school. So at this time I began to learn about student oratory and democracy and things of that sort.

And still other distractions were present to keep the student from studying. Among these was a series of assigned compositions: against tobacco and alcohol (official, automatic morality as a class chore), a description of the dawn in an imaginary little village (first step toward the journalistic practice of writing about what one doesn't know), or a defense of a foundling's rights (Red Cross sentimentality bandied about in the school). This and other foolishness made up our class in literature.

My father, worried about the milieu, used to say: "Prepare yourself for a scientific career. You will be able to do good without the fear of doing evil. In politics—and the law is, in a sense, its satellite—you will at times, without intending to, do evil things, or good things that may seem bad to others. But the opinion of others is the least important matter. You yourself will be tormented with the doubt as to whether what you do is cruel or useless, and also whether it wouldn't be worse for you not to do it. Once in the political struggle, action will be a daily torture; but not to act will be one too, and an even more excruciating one. Perhaps you would become fanatically obsessed with this or that idea and then you wouldn't have to endure this bitterness. But I wouldn't want you to be half a man, all passion and no critical judgment, and that is to be half a man. No: you would be well advised to deal with numbers, with stars, with plants, with microbes. You choose, it's up to you. But don't play with men's passions, and don't be their plaything either, my son."

The following year I became acquainted with the National Preparatory School, the great, old, traditional house on San Ildefonso Street. For my father and for me this was true happiness.

15

The National Preparatory School

A whole lifetime of perplexities ended with my enrollment, in 1922, in the National Preparatory School, where I began a period of constructive, clear thinking and the formulation of sound ideals. I entered the second-year course, although I was deficient in certain of the first-year subjects: of those that I had studied in the Colegio Mexicano, only five were accredited to my program in the Preparatory School. I remained there until 1925, studying in a leisurely fashion for my bachelor's degree. Although those were, to be sure, tumultuous times in the school, one could still absorb its glorious tradition.

It enthralled me at the outset with its monumental architectural charm. The coolness of its ample corridors, the shadows

of its colonial cloisters, the beauty of the arcades in its three
patios, the fountain in the second of these, and the quiet seclusion of the third literally possessed my eyes and my spirit. I
made an effort to arrive at the school very early or leave very
late, at those hours when it was free of students. Secondly, I
was much taken by the human element: boys from all social
classes, among whom I preferred the most unaffected, those
least resembling my companions in the Colegio Mexicano. My
father had skillfully molded my mind during the preceding
year, pointing out to me that I was not rich or privileged, and
that I should learn to live and get along with the common people. Through my companions I began to know that Mexico
City of which I had been ignorant before: the tenements of
Loreto, the slum dwellings of Peralvillo and of the Bolsa. My
teachers were not in all instances extraordinary, but an ample
and authentic environment, devoid of pretentiousness, farce,
or a concern for financial aggrandizement, enhanced them.
Then, too, there hovered over them the demanding spirits of
Gabino Barreda, master of Mexican positivism, of the Tabascan writer Manuel Sánchez Mármol, and of the illustrious
educator Justo Sierra, whose portraits I contemplated with
great emotion in the outer office of the director. Some of our
teachers were amusing, some paternal, and others marked by
singular pedagogical capacity, like don Agustín Reza, who
taught us zoology by telling us, with taste and great wit, of
the life and adventures of animals. There were methodical
ones like Maximino Martínez, who coordinated our isolated
knowledge and left us with clear and solid ideas on botany; or
amusing ones like the French teacher—don Salvador Grosso—
whose dyed mustache and inability to maintain order and silence provoked us to laughter, but who taught us enough so
that we could translate any book. Then there were tyrants
like don Elpidio López, teacher of physical geography, whose
glowering face was sufficient to prompt us to master his subject. And finally there were the young teachers, still students

in the professional schools of the University of Mexico, who brought us new socialist ideas. Among these was Dionisio Montelongo, the bald youth who in his civics class made me think that I should be a lawyer, and the three who followed one another in the Spanish language class: the Costa Rican Moisés Vincenzi, Palma Guillén, and Jesús Zavala. The last-named, however, because of the discontinuity and irregular nature of the instruction, were unable to impart very much of the program to us, although we did read *The Girls' Consent* by the Spanish dramatist Moratín, as well as essays and poems that awakened our literary ambitions. Vincenzi taught us sound Spanish Americanism; Guillén, of keen and sober mind, lectured on Spanish language and literature; Zavala conveyed a feeling for literary sensitivity, tenderness toward men and things, and valuable information on good provincial literature. It is a curious and enlightening fact that this course, so irregular in its planning, aroused more fervor in us for the literature of Mexico, Spanish America, and Spain than all the others, as a result, doubtless, of the character and enthusiasm of the participating teachers. But the classrooms began to assume a less important role, giving way to the corridors, where the most advanced boys talked of history and philosophy, and discussed texts of Nietzsche and Schopenhauer; where they read aloud the classical works that José Vasconcelos had had edited; repeated what the nervous teacher of general literature, don Erasmo Castellanos Quinto, had said about *Faust;* and praised or criticized passionately the ethics class taught at that time by a very young teacher, Vicente Lombardo Toledano.

There were also women and girls in the corridors, some of them very pretty. They were confined on the third floor of the first patio, in what we called the gynaeceum, under the vigilance of cordial governesses; but they attended classes with us and talked with the older boys at the door of the school or in the garden of Loreto Church. Some had sweethearts. I was disqualified because I was very young and still wore short pants. But far from embarrassing me as had the girls of the Colegio Mexicano, or inspiring sensual thoughts in me, the camaraderie of these young women made it possible for me to treat them without fear or desire. I liked the Russian girl Elena Boder—tiny, intelligent, and attractive, Josefina Valencia, the Reina sisters; and I admired Lucía Cortés, in my opinion the prettiest of all and my companion in the geometric drawing class. Contact with those girls, physically and scholastically more mature than I, taught me, to a certain point, to regard women in a spirit of naturalness and companionship.

A cultural tradition, an equalitarian atmosphere, plus young ladies on the scene, made me recover completely the fighting spirit and drive I had lost in the Colegio Mexicano and made it possible, too, for me to see in my father's eyes, when the courses ended, a gleam of happiness and satisfaction.

But satisfactions are short-lived.

My father always returned home at seven-thirty. Sometimes he would be a half hour late, never more, and we never sat down at the table without him. One night in December I was resting from my recently passed examinations, playing with my dog Raffles, and reading the piece of junk that Fernández y González wrote on Cervantes. I was reading a chapter on doña Guiomar, when they knocked loudly on the door. They were hard, irregular blows. My heart skipped a beat and I ran down the stairs. A drunk man and a woman were there to inform us that "a gentleman, a little old man had given them that visiting card, was ill, and had had an attack in a hotel." That was enough. I understood the terrible truth: dead, my father was dead! This was clearly written in the confusion of the poor man and woman who had brought the news; and that it was undoubtedly he was obvious from the card they had shown me. Grasping at a remote hope I reflected on their words and repeated three of them: "little old man, little old man." Because my father was not an old man. I knew that he was less than fifty; I knew from his joviality, his laugh, and the extraordinary brightness of his eyes that he was young. But they could not have been conscious of this brightness because it had been extinguished; they could only have seen his prematurely gray head. For them he was "an old fellow"; for me, my best and youngest friend.

Without my student cap that I customarily wore, I ran out to look for my cousin Juan, who lived very near to my house. I lost my voice. With faltering speech I told my aunt of the misfortune. My cousin and a Nicaraguan friend of the family accompanied me in a Ford roadster. My cousin got out at Soto Street to look for a doctor friend, Daniel Gurría, while we continued on. The Universal Hotel was a small house at the corner of Donceles and Santo Domingo Streets. My father's body was in room number 2. We had to elbow our way in. The corner bootblacks and other curiosity seekers had piled up around the door, scenting a crime. My father was lying on the bed in his shirt, face upward, his arms pillow-like under his head, his eyes cloudy and opaque. His ever-happy, deep, and lively eyes were gone forever. The friend who was with me stepped up and closed them gently.

The police inspector interrupted his work for a moment. When we arrived he was taking inventory of my father's pockets. He still wished, generously, to deceive me, assuring me, "it was just an attack, nothing more." But I had already seen the truth. Nevertheless, hope still tore at my soul and made me think of the resurrection of the flesh.

I was at the door waiting when my cousin arrived with the doctor. They informed them of the situation and the doctor, tears in his eyes, didn't wish to get out of the car. He had been my father's pupil. If his expertise was now of no avail, why see him? Standing face to face, my cousin grasped me by the shoulders and told me a number of things about the duties and responsibilities that were beginning for me, but either I couldn't or didn't want to hear them at that time. I heard other things, and very important ones, within myself: small regrets, the argument I had had with my father two days ago; the satisfaction I had given him with the success of my last examinations; the future that awaited us without money or father; the panic that I would feel at the funeral and, above all, how he had died, of what and why. Only four hours before, he had been with us, and had played and danced with my sisters. And I was obsessed with his opaque eyes, as though covered with a cloudy veil, so different from their ordinary appearance, and with his white, cold face. The weight of a grief and of a problem superior to my forces was prostrating me, destroying me. I sought solitude in the corners of the hotel, avoiding the gaze of the friends who were beginning to arrive.

With our family friend I went to notify some people and an uncle of mine, who was a congressman, of what had happened, and then I went home. In the meantime my mother and my aunt Cristina had gone to the hotel and learned the truth. At eleven o'clock at night they brought the body to the house on a stretcher. My father was laid out in my parents' room. In mine they put the surplus furniture and this prevented my closing the door. As a result I had no place to hide. I was distressed by the moans of my sisters, by the silent grief of my mother, and, far from consoling me, by the *pro forma* condolences of casual acquaintances and the compassionate phrases of my intimate friends who patted me reassuringly on the head. "Just when you needed him most," don Luis Graham said to me. It was horrible when they took the body away the next day, but it was a relief.

There wasn't an empty spot in the house. Wreaths, wreaths, and more wreaths! My father was a magistrate at that time and the courts arranged the funeral; the great army of his friends did the rest. The coffin was austerely plain but, even so, too elegant for a man who all his life had scorned elegance. He would have laughed at the silk bolsters and lining, and the velvet. His human understanding would have tolerated the responses of a priest whom it was necessary to admit to the house because he was accompanied by a magistrate friend of my father, the former intent on ensuring my father's ultramundane happiness; but perhaps he would have rejected the novenary, that proved so useful to the lovemakers. For nine nights the men talked of politics, the women of births and cooking, and the young people of love. Everyone irritated me except a lady who continually forgot the "Blessed be the sacred fruit of Thy womb, Jesus," and who, although she wheezed mechanically through the tiresome prayer, touched me deeply, to the point of tears.

I knew and loved my father so much that I could imagine his attitude toward any event. His reaction to those prayers would have been expressed in an indulgent smile. I remembered a frequent phrase of his: "When I'm pushing up daisies." His reference to death could not have been simpler or more beautiful. Nothing of heaven or hell, but neither the harsh image of worms.

A phrase spoken by an orator at his tomb is the only thing to which he would have subscribed from among everything that followed his death: "The wealth of his integrity is today the poverty of his home." And he would have been greatly tormented by the exact and material truth of the phrase, by thoughts of the hard times awaiting us. In his brief death agony that had been, without doubt, his greatest torture, loving father that he was.

On the same night as the funeral we went to live in the house of my cousins. Three months later, when certain creditors made payments and the Obregón government, through the courts to which my father belonged, established a pension for the family, we moved to a little house in the San Rafael district.

A pseudo friend, an uncle of mine and former partner of my father, gave me one of my first lessons on the human condition. I accused him, perhaps unjustifiably, of having appropriated certain monies owed us. In any event, within two weeks after my father's death he had changed; he reprehended me over the loss of one of his books, and managed our affairs in a very desultory manner. During my father's lifetime, however, he had been as meek as a lamb. My father, who privately accused him of being a venal professional man and public official, had always treated him with harshness and he always obeyed. He and others quickly taught me all the lessons about life that I hadn't learned in the Preparatory School.

I lived introverted, embittered, and lonely. My house, more modest than ever, was situated on a small, private street in a humble quarter. There my mother was to sigh and my sisters languish. I harbored such great animosity that I came to think that a friend of the family who was a professional rival of my father, and whom the latter, because of his greater worth, overshadowed, might in some way have been to blame for his death. The *Democrat*, a scandal sheet which, at the time of my father's death, published an article insinuating the possibility of a crime, had set me to thinking on this track. Besides, my wild, fifteen-year-old imagination was at work. I was discovering some strange facts: my father's integrity had been a hindrance to some; the wallet he was carrying at the time of his death and which contained important documents, had disappeared. Furthermore, the cause of his death had never been perfectly clarified. He was exceptionally vigorous and was suffering from no illness. It is to be assumed that he felt ill in his office, that he left with the idea of going home and that, feeling much worse on reaching the street, entered the first hotel he came across. Sentimental pressures prevented an autopsy. An embolism? Angina pectoris? The latter, the death certificate said. Abandoned and hurt as I felt myself to be, without sufficient experience to understand and pardon human defects; with a fifteen-year-old's imagination; aware of the position my father was about to occupy and of the corruption of the many who coveted it, I was caught up in a welter of doubts, mistrust, and fear. My father was still with me every moment:

they had remodeled his suits for me; I was carrying his watch; I read his books and papers, even the most confidential ones. Thus I came to know him better than ever—then I suffered more than ever.

This was a grief that could be alleviated only in my studies, in my school, and I dedicated myself to them with body and soul. Besides my mother and sisters, I had no other love than the Preparatory School.

16

Disenchantment

I was now independent: the only son of a widow, and with two loving sisters, I felt myself—somewhat conceitedly—to be the head of the family. But the political or, more accurately, apolitical posture of my late father cast its shadow over my thoughts. In a material sense I now enjoyed the great freedom and autonomy of an orphan; but spiritually I was still under his influence. This was the case even more than when he was alive; for his death elevated him in stature in my eyes, sanctified him. I was free now to tell my companions, without the reticence one feels extolling the living, of countless acts of heroism and abnegation performed during his exemplary existence. His friends as well as his enemies spoke of his unimpeachable integrity as one speaks of a legend. I had more in-

formation about him now than ever: about how he broke with
the governor of Tabasco because he tried to suborn him in the
matter of a judicial decision that my father had rendered
against him; how General Díaz tried to have him transferred
to the judicature of Veracruz and thus give the Governor a
free hand; how he hid Pedro, his rebel friend, in his house. I
learned of his recent attitude as a public official, upright to a
fault, and maintaining a posture of mute but intense criticism
of the immorality of the public administration that surrounded
him. Of course his opinions were sacred to me, and I set out to
discover their bases. I read the works of the political thinker
Emilio Rabasa, as well as those of the controversial writer
Francisco Bulnes and became more of a Porfirista than ever.
In the Preparatory School I engaged in a continuous and, for
me, most useful discussion with my discerning young teacher
of economics, Ramón Beteta; I had a dispute with a general's
nephew because he attacked the old Porfirista regime; I felt
myself being interpreted when I heard my Latin teacher, don
Luis Betancourt, say that he was a reactionary and proud of
it; I formed intimate friendships with the sons of honorable
and discontented revolutionaries and detested the sons of corrupt rebels. In my view the fathers of the latter were simply
thieves who owned expensive automobiles; traitors who had
liquidated their leaders and their friends, driven by an ob-
sessive desire for command; ignoramuses who knew nothing
either of the military expertise implicit in their army rank or
of the ideals to which they gave fulsome praise in their toasts;
plunderers who were selling their country piece by piece to
the Yankees; cynical "revolutionaries" who rubbed elbows
with the old aristocracy that had thrived "taking advantage of
the honesty of don Porfirio." On my desk I placed a picture
of my father and, above it, a very large one—occupying almost half the wall—illuminated and resplendent with its med-
als, of General Porfirio Díaz. But, seated in his presidential
chair, don Porfirio couldn't help seeing all the books that

passed through my hands and how, little by little, they were undermining my worship of him.

I was a defender of the poor. I was familiar with the ideas of my maternal grandfather in this regard and felt an obligation to dedicate my own efforts to the same struggle; I recalled my father's honest existence and aspired to duplicate it. The men who had been involved with constitutional reform, the Juárez group, were the ones who inspired my greatest admiration. They had defended their native soil and the rights of the people against foreigners and cruel overseers. I felt the need for a movement that would cleanse the Revolution of its blemishes and its corruptors. This was not a reactionary ideology or sensibility. I liked don Porfirio—I explained to my friends, surprised or annoyed by my, for them, strange Porfirista partisanship—because he had not stolen from the public treasury; because after thirty years of leadership he left Mexico with only a modest fortune, whereas some of the do-nothing generals of his time made hundreds of thousands of dollars in a few days; because he had risked his life defending the country against the attacks of priests, aristocrats, and foreigners. I loved the patriotic and honorable don Porfirio extolled by my family circle, the don Porfirio whom I considered good and virtuous. My love for the people, for the country, and for certain democratic principles, enhanced during a year's reading in Mexican history, made me see a leader in don Porfirio. My surroundings and schooling had been such that I was unable to see that he had yielded before foreign imperialism, although he had fought heroically, as I had learned, on April 2, 1867, against the French; that he had abandoned the Indian and fashioned his political program on a fawning admiration of Europe, despite his humble social origin and his mixture of Indian blood; that he had been, wittingly or unwittingly, an instrument of organized social injustice, ages old.

In this welter of errors it is understandable that I assumed all sorts of extreme positions. During the struggle in 1923 between the Preparatory School, whose director was the young socialist leader Vicente Lombardo Toledano, and the Secretary of Public Education, José Vasconcelos, I didn't take sides because, since both were public officials identified with the Revolution, neither aroused any enthusiasm in me. And when a group of students, incipient barbarians incited by reactionary foolishness, marked the murals—revolutionary in theme and technique—of José Clemente Orozco and Diego Rivera, I didn't feel the least indignation.

It was not my classes that opened my eyes. Few of my teachers had clearly defined ideologies. I did have two who were practicing Catholics, but through economic necessity they were always careful not to touch on the theme of the Church's opposition to the Revolution, an indiscretion that would have cost them their jobs. It was not, as I say, the classes, but the companions who chatted in the corridors and published student newspapers, and it was, too, the atmosphere of the street.

In 1923, shortly after a strike at the Preparatory School, a young Juchitecan Indian, nephew of an irreproachable leader assassinated in Oaxaca, asked me to contribute an article to a newspaper that his group was going to establish. This was the most revolutionary group in the school: it was made up of boys from the laboring classes or from families with a revolutionary background. On that account they saw the virtues of the Revolution more clearly than I. This was doubtless one of the first groups to speak in the Preparatory School of the Russian Revolution. Why did they feel in harmony with me? How did they know me? It was probably because I had presided over some stormy meetings of Tabascans attending the school—meetings that caused a sensation; I wrote in all the student papers; I had won a history competition. Was it that they knew me as a "revolutionary Porfirista"—a Porfirista as regards what were, or what I thought to be, don Porfirio's good qualities; a revolutionary through a sentiment that was naturally rather formless and vague? At that time I wrote an article called "Mexico and Socialism," which appeared, as a matter of great pride to me, on page one of the first number of *Avalanche*—the frightful name of my revolutionary friends' newspaper—beside an editorial in which they asked that Lombardo Toledano be named Minister of Public Education. My article was brave and impassioned, in keeping with the paper's epigraph: "We shall go, torch in hand, to set fire to the brothel of the powerful." My article was, above all, rebellious, and then, too, it was liberal, socialistic, communistic, and anarchistic, all at the same time. It abridged the French Revolution and the three Internationals. In one of its final paragraphs it said: "Let us adore Lenin, Trotsky, and Chicherin." I had just read *The New Times* by the Argentine essayist José Ingenieros, the only thing that had come into my hands about red Russia, as well as the text of a debate between two North American professors on socialism. I also read a few books by Henry George, whom my father had read frequently, and *The Struggle for Bread* by Kropotkin. And so I cited Kropotkin along with Marx and Lunacharsky, mixing anarchists and Communists. In that potpourri there were only three positive items: a determined and youthful hatred of exploiters, an exalted and passionate love for the oppressed, and the decision to dedicate my life to their defense.

Later the voices of the clan again reached my ears. In 1923 my cousin Juan joined the insurrection that don Adolfo de la Huerta, Secretary of the Treasury and presidential candidate, led against the support being given by President Alvaro Obregón to the candidacy of General Plutarco Elías Calles, Minister of War. At this time I again sought the friendship of Juan's mother and brothers, greatly distressed during the whole of this adventure. I refused to have any more contact with my revolutionary companions of *Avalanche;* I repudiated them because they had enrolled in the Obregón Student Center and had attended a banquet with General Obregón.

Like many youths of the time, embued with the ideals of the French and North American revolutions, living fully the democratic dream, I was against Obregón because I believed him to have rigged the vote in favor of his friend Calles. But I didn't join the other side either, because among the followers of don Adolfo de la Huerta I saw as many professional politicians as in the other group. The situation in my own province finally swayed me in favor of don Adolfo. I had become convinced that the governor of Tabasco, the revolutionary leader Dimas, was fatal for my state and for the country, and I never stopped attacking him, although his uncle, a close friend of my father's, had awarded me a scholarship for my studies. And I was further influenced by my admiration for my young cousin who, already an attorney, occupied positions of responsibility and danger at the side of de la Huerta—Under Secretary of the Interior and Governor of Campeche—and who, upon Obregón's military triumph, wandered through the forests of Tabasco, Chiapas, and Guatemala with Generals Salvador Alvarado and Cándido Aguilar, initiators of the Revolution of 1910. My political posture was again being shaped by the Foucher clan and by an indelible admiration for the epic, the bellicose, and the heroic.

On one of my visits to my aunt's home I had a great encounter: with Dr. Manuel Mestre Ghigliazza, at that time Director of the Mexican National Library. He was a former Maderist leader and Governor of Tabasco and a friend, from childhood, of my mother's family. More than anything a poet and a journalist, he carried on a long and romantic, that is to say, essentially ineffective, struggle against the dictatorship of General Porfirio Díaz. He attacked this administration from the year 1904. His actions transcended the boundaries of the province, and his articles were eagerly sought after by the press of the Yucatán Peninsula and even that of the capital. He was one of the best collaborators on *The Third Empire*, an anti-Díaz newspaper, and one of the provincial companions of

Filomeno Mata and Inocencio Arriola, early leaders of the revolution against Díaz. A member of one of the most respected families of Tabasco, the son of a governor, relative of a minister, a physician graduated from the Faculty of Medicine of the capital, married to a woman of social position in Campeche, he refused many tempting offers, such as a seat in the Chamber of Representatives of the Díaz government. He was one of the anti-Porfiristas through absolute and disinterested conviction. He could have attained the highest level of power in the dictatorship but he refused; he could have reaped honors and he eschewed them. He was one of the men of high station of the time who put his intelligence to the service of the people. Of French intellectual formation, translator of French poets, the doctor was an heir to the ideals of the French Revolution of 1789. An intellectual, essentially a litterateur, he did not owe his renown to action, for which he had neither a liking nor qualifications of any kind, but to his intelligence, to his literary and historical culture, unequaled in Tabasco and scarcely rivaled throughout the country. A man of romantic legend, a Don Juan, emotive and sensual among a people in whom emotion and sensuality are enhanced by a propitious land and climate, white—part Catalan, part Italian blood—he did not guide the people of Tabasco but seduced them as he might have a woman. But this he did not do for his pleasure or profit. The doctor, in addition to having many talents and charms, was a man of firm liberal convictions and irreproachable economic and political integrity.

A worldly man, he presented a ready target for his enemies. He was imprisoned various times, took part in meetings, and was elevated, despite himself, to the category of leader, which displeased him because he knew he couldn't be one. He realized that, being, as he was, somewhat of a dilettante in revolutionary matters, he lacked the courage and profound faith in his people and in his country that such an undertaking required. With the fall of Díaz he was elected governor of Tabasco amidst the love and enthusiastic acclaim of the masses. The doctor is one of the best examples of the intellectual in the liberal revolution: besieged by the powerful, a man of the pen and not of the sword, finding himself in violent circumstances, he saw his rule turn to misrule. When Madero was assassinated, through the treachery of Victoriano Huerta, he did not take up arms, either because of the risks or because of his limitations as a political leader, although he denounced the crime in a speech. Huerta summoned the doctor to the capital and prohibited him from leaving it. Carranza, less cultured and more energetic than the doctor, never liked him. Obregón, who had the discernment to estimate intelligence and learning in order to use them for his own benefit, offered him high posts when he reached the presidency. The doctor, discouraged by the poverty and exclusion he had endured during the Carranza years, convinced that the Revolution had not ushered in the liberal paradise of which he had dreamed so candidly, refused the important compromising posts and accepted only a niche: the directorship of the National Library. There he could devote himself to his historical curiosities, live with dust and moths, and become as old physically as he was beginning to be in political sagacity. But, still crying out against social injustice and public immorality, his voice preserved youthful accents.

He was the best friend of my youth, more like a brother than a father. Extraordinarily intelligent, with an exceptionally keen mind, a true tactician of human relations, he knew how to talk to me in my language, which was a mixture of enthusiasm for noble causes, Porfirista tradition, and Tabascan passion. We coincided on the first point; we might have clashed on the second but did not; and we differed on the last. Moreover, the doctor had another weapon at his disposal for correcting my reactionary point of view: the library. The books he lent me were as fruitful as his unforgettable conversation.

After knowing **Dr.** Mestre for two months, I had become a
fervent admirer of Madero's, as a result of his great admiration
for him. My surroundings had originally given me the impression that he was a cheap demagogue who disturbed the peace
and prosperity of Mexico by opposing General Díaz. How
wrong I had been! The goodness of this pure man brought me
to tears; his sacrifice made me wish to shout. How was it possible that I had lived so long without being aware of his moral
stature? Ah, but that was not all: I once heard an uncle of
mine say that the day Madero was assassinated was like a holi-
day for him. At that time I prepared a bibliography on the
Revolution. The doctor furnished the books, and I read them
very carefully. Now I was not only a Maderist: I was a liberal, a French liberal. On that account I couldn't be a Carrancista or a Zapatista, much less a Villista, because all three of
these men had, in my inflamed and biased judgment, disre-
garded basic human rights. And still less could I be an Obregonista or Callista and support the groups then in power,
which I considered abusers of the ballot, full of captains of industry who were selling us to the Yankee bankers through the
Bucareli treaty of 1923, covering subsoil rights and contrary
to the Constitution of 1917. But then I found out, too, that
the Revolution had supported sacred principles and that I had
drunk—without knowing it—of its waters, because my father's
consideration for the people and his faith in democracy, ideas
which I had absorbed from him, coincided with the aims of
the Revolution. I learned also that it had saints, leaders, and
ideologists who deserved more admiration than don Porfirio.

I knew very little about Russia or the Russian Revolution.
I read Spanish and Spanish-American literature, both old and
new. In such writers as Pérez Galdós and Blasco Ibáñez my
anticlericalism was refined; in Valera I relished literary grace;
in Pereda I recaptured love for the province. In Leopoldo
Alas, in the Cuban writer Emilio Bobadilla (Fray Candil), and
in Luis Bonafoux I learned the techniques of opposition litera-

ture that I was going to use later against Dimas, the revolutionary governor of Tabasco. And even in the copious and disordered culture of Bobadilla I gleaned knowledge about everything—formless and vague but nevertheless rich and multiple incentives to further learning, and I came to know something about Cuba and all of America. Bobadilla, because he had lived in Spain, had a global view of the Continent. My study of Bobadilla, who was markedly Francophile, led me, curiously enough, to an interest in the two figures I most admired during my adolescence, the two great Spanish-American patriots Simón Bolívar and José Martí, and gave me some knowledge of the literary and political life of Spain.

In the Preparatory School we edited a newspaper, *Agora*, in which we simultaneously took some first literary steps and annoyed our companions and teachers. Other boys' literary works were the targets of two sections I had in the paper—critical articles inspired by my readings of the Spanish writer Clarín and the Cuban Bobadilla. The school was undergoing a crisis at that time. The new director, a doctor, seemed able to direct his attention only to sports and setting-up exercises. The flagstones of the school's central patio were stained with blood on one occasion from a savage boxing match. North American influence, seemingly accepted in its defects and rejected in the area of its merits, reached such an extreme that this old cultural establishment was the scene of the most barbarous sports. At the same time, other sports were developed, which were more useful, noble, and healthful; these kept the youth from vice and venereal disease and even taught them to bathe, but these were overdone, at the expense of teaching.

The superficiality of the Colegio Mexicano extended to the Preparatory School. Classes deteriorated. The teachers got worse and worse, and the good ones, their attention monopolized by politics, attended classes only rarely. We studied by ourselves as best we could, with all the confusion and errors inherent in self-instruction. It was then that I discovered the famous Venezuelan poet and critic Rufino Blanco-Fombona, successor in my sanctum to Emilio Bobadilla. Blanco-Fombona, a violent Venezuelan who struggled against the dictator Juan Vicente Gómez, as I did against Dimas, was bound to captivate my Tabascan passions. Fortunately, he acquainted me further with Spanish literature; gave me an understanding of Spanish-American authors such as Lugones, Herrera Reissig, and Santos Chocano; and indirectly turned my attention to Spanish-American classical writers such as Sarmiento and Montalvo. The books of the Mexican historian Carlos Pereyra led me, a little later, to an understanding of the history of the Continent and to a greater love for Spain, developing in me—a compensation for the inevitable Hispanophobia of my childhood—an anachronistic kind of Hispanism, racial in nature, and a sentimental anti-imperialism directed against both Britain and the United States. A rather disorderly reading of such Spanish writers as Menéndez y Pelayo, Pi y Margall, and Joaquín Costa enlarged my stores of information on my beloved Spanish history and literature.

The students' culture received yet another blow, more lethal than the boxing matches: the oratorical contests. In these the contestants had first to deliver a prepared discourse, "the prepared improvisation," and then to improvise further on any topic that the jury fired at them. The themes, most ample in scope, fell like missiles on those tender brains, on those embryonic cultures: "The Mexican Revolution as a Social Phenomenon," "The Monroe Doctrine," "Greek Culture," "Christianity as Superior Philosophy and Ethics," "American Cross-Breeding," and so on. The adolescents would string commonplace after commonplace, acquiring enough nerve to disgorge them later in public, and at the conclusion would emit a few memorized high-sounding gems, deliberately nebulous so that they could be utilized for any subject, as appropriate for one thing as for another. In this way intellectual irresponsibility was fostered among Mexican youth. And, because there were no other kinds of competition, and the prizes in oratory were very tempting—trips to Europe and the United States, and attendant publicity much sought after by the conceited youth—no young Mexican escaped the seduction of this frivolous test. There were intelligent, even brilliant, students who wasted their literary sensibility in the vanity of these contests, as well as others whom the hope of noisy triumph separated from orderly and fruitful study. If there were some who withstood their victory and preserved their intellectual promise, they were the exceptions. These competitions were a factory of flippancy, superficiality, loquaciousness, intellectual poverty, and demagoguery of the worst sort. Although I despised them, I too was tempted by the dreamed-of trip to Europe, and, one night when I was racked by a 102-degree fever, I began to prepare two speeches—on José Martí and Simón Bolívar. But my fear of the public and my then uncontrollable nervousness saved me from participating in that oratorical farce.

During the last year of Preparatory School, the philosophy classes, taught with great enthusiasm by José Romano Muñoz and Samuel Ramos, opened new horizons to us. And, in the third term of the general history course, we acquired much objective knowledge, very useful for an understanding of the events then shaping the world. In that course, we began to investigate by ourselves.

Unfortunately, there was no real order or arrangement in the teaching. We were under the influence of frightened Catholics, half-Protestants, stormy liberals, and, at times, insecure and nebulous socialists.

No one oriented us. We continued to be swayed by passions and personality cults. For people like our teachers, dependent on the budget for their living, it was extremely difficult to make an objective analysis of the Mexican potpourri. We lived in a welter of words, in an ocean of falsehoods, in a whirlwind of contradictions.

A problem was floating about in my head with which I was

reluctant to come to grips: don Porfirio. I no longer mentioned him. I no longer liked to hear either my relatives speak of him with enthusiasm or my companions refer to him with hatred. But his portrait remained in its place over my desk, like an appendix, remnant of a remote, dead past.

This would not last for long. One day a companion from *Avalanche* came to visit me. There were other visitors in the living room; in my room, don Porfirio's picture. I couldn't invite my friend to go up. I was ashamed and remorseful. I was no longer a Porfirista.

For the first time my mother spoke to me adversely of don Porfirio: "He had not been a saint." In her mind were memories of those assassinated in Veracruz, of the journalists killed throughout Mexico, of the violent deaths of Generals Corona and García de la Cadena.

One day I took down the portrait, removed it from the frame, rolled it up, and placed it behind my wardrobe. Shortly afterward, some friend of the family carried it off.

This was a cycle that was coming to an end. My activities now overflowed the boundaries of the school and were, at the same time, an epilogue to the inquisitive existence of the child and a prologue to the agitated and grievous life of the man.

Glossary

Political and Military Figures

AGUILAR, CÁNDIDO (1888–1960). Son-in-law and supporter of Venustiano Carranza in the latter's struggle against Victoriano Huerta. In 1923 he participated in the de la Huerta insurrection against Alvaro Obregón.

ALVARADO, SALVADOR (1879–1924). Important ideologist of the Revolution and a supporter of Francisco I. Madero and Carranza in their struggle against Porfirio Díaz and Victoriano Huerta. He took part in the unsuccessful insurrection of Adolfo de la Huerta against Obregón, and in 1924 was the victim of a treacherous ambush while still fighting against the latter near the Guatemalan border.

CALLES, PLUTARCO ELÍAS (1877–1945). Opponent of Díaz and Victoriano Huerta; President of the Republic (1924–28). His administration is remembered for the consolidation of important political and social reforms.

CARRANZA, VENUSTIANO (1859–1920). Leader of the insurrection against Victoriano Huerta at the time Madero was assassinated; President of the Republic (1917–20), his term ended by assassination. Carranza symbolizes the legal triumph of the Revolution. Although of high social position, he supported the aims of the people for a wide range of advanced social reforms, incorporated in the Constitution of 1917, which, with some modifications, is still in force today.

HUERTA, ADOLFO DE LA (1881–1954). Opponent of Díaz and Victoriano Huerta (no relation); Provisional President in 1920; in 1923, a candidate for the presidency and leader of the unsuccessful uprising against Obregón.

HUERTA, VICTORIANO (1845–1916). Military figure, President Madero's Chief-of-Staff. In 1913 he betrayed Madero, imprisoned him in the National Palace, and had him assassinated days later together with Vice-President José María Pino Suárez. He was President of the Republic (1913–14) and was unseated by a new popular uprising; he died in exile.

MADERO, FRANCISCO I. (1873–1913). Leader of the 1911 national uprising against the Díaz dictatorship. A wealthy farmer educated in France and in the United States, he led, in 1910, the most important democratic campaign for the presidency in Mexican history but was defeated through election frauds that retained General Díaz in office. After the uprising, he was elected President (1911) and remained in office until February, 1913, when he was assassinated by order of Victoriano Huerta.

OBREGÓN, ALVARO (1880–1928). Carranza's most important military leader. He defeated Francisco Villa when the latter rebelled against the legal authority of Carranza; he succeeded Carranza as President of the Republic (1920–24). Re-elected in 1928, he was murdered some days later.

VILLA, FRANCISCO (1878–1923). Better known as Pancho Villa, a supporter of Madero and Carranza against the dictatorships of Díaz and Victoriano Huerta. An extremely talented military organizer, Villa was the key figure, as Chief of the Northern Division, in the annihilation of the army that supported the Díaz and Victoriano Huerta dictatorships. He is a prominent figure in the Mexican popular epic.

ZAPATA, EMILIANO (1879–1919). Peasant leader from the state of Morelos, revered in Mexico as the symbol of agrarianism, of land and freedom for the people. He joined the revolutionary movement first in 1911 with Madero, and again in 1913 with Carranza and Villa; he was a fierce opponent of Díaz and Victoriano Huerta.

Foreign Words (Spanish Unless Otherwise Indicated)

bona nit (Catalan). Good evening
campechano. Native of Campeche; frank, cheerful, cordial
canoa campechana. Campechan cargo boat

cantina. Saloon and provision store

centavo. Cent

colegio. Elementary school

crianza. Hanger-on, extra member of the family

criollo. Mexican of Spanish descent

don, doña. Titles of respect prefixed to Christian name of a gentleman or lady

guacho. On Mexico's Gulf Coast, designation for the inhabitants of the central part of the country

hacienda. Large estate

Instituto Juárez. Institution of higher learning, which offered college courses, law and other professional training

jícama. Aqueous, onion-shaped root, ordinarily eaten raw with salt and lemon

jota. Aragonese dance

kam pech (Mayan). A place of snakes and chiggers

mestizo. In Mexico, one of mixed Spanish and Indian blood

monsieur (French). Sir, gentleman

mosiú, mushú. Corruptions of the French word *monsieur*

niño. Familiar appellation used by servants in addressing their masters; literally, "boy," "child"

pan de cazón. Layers of corn *tortillas* and dogfish or sand shark meat

panucho. Small, fried *tortilla* filled with beans, onion, and fish

peso. Dollar; Mexican monetary unit: 100 centavos

playón. Large shore or beach

Porfirismo. Support of Porfirio Díaz; reverence for his memory

San. Saint (used before masculine proper names)

sierra. Mountain ridge of irregular outline; mountain region

siesta. Short, midday rest

taco. Small *tortilla*, rolled and filled with meat, chicken, cheese, etc.

toquilla. Knit lining worn under the hat as a protection against perspiration stains

tortilla. Thin, flat, unleavened corn cake

totoposte. In Tabasco, large, thin variety of toasted *tortilla*

tuncuruxú (Mayan). Owl; see page 61

tusa. Burrowing field rat

Special Terms

Callista. Pertaining to, or a supporter of, Plutarco Elías Calles

Carrancista. Pertaining to, or a supporter of, Venustiano Carranza

Dominguista. Pertaining to, or a supporter of, Luis Felipe Domínguez

Maderista. Pertaining to, or a supporter of, Francisco I. Madero

Obregonista. Pertaining to, or a supporter of, Alvaro Obregón

Porfirista. Pertaining to, or a supporter of, Porfirio Díaz

Villista. Pertaining to, or a supporter of, Francisco Villa

Zapatista. Pertaining to, or a supporter of, Emiliano Zapata